RAILWAY AND TRAMWAY BODIES

ANOTHER LIFE

Royston Morris

AMBERLEY

This book is dedicated to the fond memory of Brenda Valerie Mitchell,
a truly wonderful warm-hearted, loving, caring and generous wife, mother and grandmother.
10 May 1943 to 25 June 2018.

First published 2019

Amberley Publishing
The Hill, Stroud,
Gloucestershire, GL5 4EP

www.amberley-books.com

ISBN: 978 1 4456 8429 1 (print)
ISBN: 978 1 4456 8430 7 (ebook)

British Library Cataloguing in Publication Data.
A catalogue record for this book is available from the British Library.

Typeset in 9pt on 12pt Celeste.
Origination by Amberley Publishing.
Printed in the UK.

Contents

Introduction

During the First World War, there were a minimum of 120 different railway companies that were operating in the UK, all of which were under the control of the government.

Under Prime Minister David Lloyd George, a white paper was produced in 1920, suggesting that the railway network should fall into five regions: Southern, Western, Eastern, North Western and North Eastern, with London having a separate group and Scotland and Ireland having single groupings. Following on from many protests – mostly from the Scottish companies, who expressed a wish to be included within the English regions – this proposal was abolished and the government finally decided that the individual companies would be grouped together under four railway companies. The four companies (often referred to as the Big Four) would be known as:

- The Great Western Railway, covering from London to Cornwall and up to the Midlands, as well as the majority of Wales.
- The Southern Railway, covering the southern part of the country from London to Cornwall and the whole of Kent.
- The London, Midland & Scottish Railway, covering London, the Midlands and the western side of Scotland.
- The London & North Eastern Railway, covering London and the counties of Norfolk, Suffolk and Essex, as well as the entire eastern side of the country, all the way up to Inverness and the Scottish Highlands.

This led to the passing of the Railways Act 1921 (or Grouping Act), which would come into effect on 1 January 1923. Following this grouping the four new companies found themselves in possession of numerous items of rolling stock, much of which was very old and would be in need of expensive repairs, so they each decided independently to sell off these items for scrap.

It is unknown which scrap merchant or dealer came up with the idea of selling the bodies of these vehicles to the public so that they could be used as summer houses, animal shelters, store sheds, etc. However, the trend soon caught on and the bodies of hundreds of vehicles began appearing all over the country. In some cases where the carriages were concerned, the buyer would purchase directly from the railway company, who would pay for the transportation – providing the destination was a reasonable distance from the works, depot or yard where the vehicle had been purchased from.

During the time of Barbara Castle as Minister of Transport in the late 1960s, due to the Beeching Cuts which led to over 2,000 miles of railways across the country being closed, British Rail had several thousand vehicles (mainly freight) that had to be disposed of. These were sold to scrap merchants across the country and the bodies were rapidly sold to the public, and many can still be seen dotted across the countryside to this day.

The railway companies were not alone in selling on the bodies of redundant vehicles; several tramway companies also sold tramcars to the public. Unlike the railway carriages, these bodies were rarely used as living accommodation, but instead tended to end up as chicken houses and bus shelters.

This book features some of the numerous bodies that have seen years of further use after their working days were finished, and also some of those that have been rescued and restored to their former glory on preserved heritage railways or at museums.

CHAPTER 1

Pre-Grouping Passenger Carriages

Companies Amalgamated into the Great Western Railway (GWR)

When the Grouping of the railways took place in January 1923, one of the Big Four was not a new company: the Great Western Railway, which had been formed in 1833. With Grouping, the GWR found it had acquired some forty-three individual railway companies – more than the other three put together, although the vast majority of those were very small, with little or hardly any rolling stock. Moreover, in the years preceding this, approximately eighty-seven smaller companies had already been absorbed into the existing GWR.

The Great Western Railway came to own some 1,500 carriages from its incorporated companies, which were added to its own stock. The passenger-carrying vehicles of only nine of those companies are currently known to exist as grounded bodies (although there may be others that have not yet been discovered). Of the nine, the main three companies whose stock still survive to this day are the Barry, Cambrian and Taff Vale railways.

In 1884, the Barry Dock & Railway Company was incorporated into the Barry Railway. Although it was a railway that was mainly used for carrying coal and minerals, it did run a suburban passenger service between Cardiff and Barry. Built at the Ashbury Railway Carriage & Iron Company in Manchester in 1896 this was a six-wheeled, six-compartment, third-class carriage. Initially numbered 45, it was later taken into the GWR fleet and re-numbered 465.

Withdrawn in 1928, it became a bungalow in Starcross, Devon. In 1985 it was preserved by members of the West Somerset Railway Association and moved to their base at Williton, where it was pictured on 30 September 1995, some ten years after being purchased, still awaiting restoration work to begin. By 2000 it had been moved to the Vale of Glamorgan Railway and mounted onto the underframe of a LNER six-wheeled goods brake van. Following the closure of the VoG Railway, the body was removed from the underframe. It currently resides at a private residence in Powys, Wales.

The Bristol & Exeter Railway opened in stages between 1841 and 1844, and was renowned for its drawn-out and expensive 'Gauge War' with the London & South Western Railway in the mid-1840s. Both it and the original GWR had Isambard Kingdom Brunel as their Chief Engineer, and they both used Brunel's preferred broad gauge of 7 feet, as opposed to the now standard 4 feet 8.5 inches. Both companies vied for the rights to run lines to the same area, but at that time Parliament would only allow one line from one company to serve a particular area. The 'Gauge War' was finally resolved in 1854, when Brunel and the GWR were forced out of necessity to change their lines to 4 feet 8.5 inches, uniting the entire rail network with a single, standardised gauge.

The B&ER was amalgamated into the original GWR in 1876, and its vehicles are extremely rare. This example was built at Lawrence Hill in Bristol by the Bristol Wagon & Carriage Company in 1875 as either a four- or six-wheeled, six-compartment, non-corridored vehicle, numbered 8. It was re-numbered to 1166 after amalgamation with the GWR and was withdrawn in 1906. It is pictured in use as a workshop/storage shed at a former nursery just outside Bath on 12 July 2013.

The Cambrian Railways had its main works in Oswestry in Shropshire, and in 1889 that was where this four-wheeled, two-compartment director's saloon, No. 9, was built. It was re-numbered 418 by the GWR in 1923 and it was downgraded to a third-class vehicle and used as a football saloon. In 1936 it was withdrawn from service, sold and moved to Steanbow on the end of a train consist mounted onto a flatbed wagon.

Upon arrival at the level crossing in Steanbow, the body was removed from the wagon by a waiting crane and transfered into a farm wagon with a tractor on it. The body was taken about 100 yards down the road from the level crossing and was put into the side of a field, where it would serve as a family home until the early 1950s. After this period it was used by local tramps who worked as casual farm labourers during times of harvest, before becoming home to sheep and goats in the 1980s and '90s. It was photographed in situ on 28 December 1996, in the same position that it had been placed some sixty years earlier. In 2005 the body was purchased for restoration and it was replaced by another vehicle (*see Chapter 16*). It is currently under cover in dry storage at an unknown location.

The Cambrian Railways was formed in 1864 when the four biggest companies in Mid-Wales were amalgamated into one. Further amalgamations occurred in 1865 and 1904, which gave the new company over 230 miles of line through a vast area of the Welsh countryside. This six-wheeled, six-compartment, third-class carriage, No. 247, was built in Birmingham by the Metropolitan C&W Co. in 1895. Becoming GWR No. 4106 in 1923, it remained in service for a further ten years, until 1933. The body was then sold and taken to the garden of a house in Appleton, near Oxford, where it was discovered in 1994. Now in two halves, it was purchased and taken to the preserved Chinnor & Princes Risborough Railway, where the halves were reunited and put onto the platform at Risborough station, where it sees use as a buffet and waiting room. It was photographed there on 16 September 2013.

This vehicle was one of a batch of ten second-hand bogie vehicles purchased from the MR, being constructed in 1895 at Derby, and was a five-compartment luggage brake composite. It was acquired by the Midland & South Western Junction Railway in 1909 and re-numbered to 64 (the original MR numbers are unknown, as they were re-numbered very rapidly, often on the same day as their purchase). In 1924 it was re-numbered by the GWR to No. 6367. Following its withdrawal from service in 1930, the body was taken to Bowling Green in Cornwall, where it was used as a bungalow until the mid-2000s, when it was removed due to the owner wanting to build an extension. It was then taken about half a mile away to Lavrean, where it awaits conversion into summer accommodation, and it was here that it was photographed on 14 June 2014.

The Rhondda & Swansea Bay Railway was one of three companies (the other two being the Port Talbot and the South Wales Mineral railways) that effectively came under the GWR many years prior to the amalgamation in January 1923. In the case of the R&SBR, this happened as early as 1906, when the company's rolling stock was sent to Swindon for repair, and therefore the GWR was deemed to be the parent company. Built in 1895 at the Ashbury Railway Carriage & Iron Company for the Rhondda & Swansea Bay Railway, this eight-wheeled, seven-compartment, third-class coach, No. 72, was re-numbered in May 1923 to 4223 following the amalgamation. Remaining in service for ten more years, it was withdrawn in September 1933. The body was sold and taken to Inches, near Bodmin, and became a bungalow named Swinden Villa (note the incorrect spelling). It was still being used as such during my visit there on 19 June 2011.

Companies Amalgamated into the London, Midland & Scottish Railway (LMS)

The London, Midland & Scottish Railway was formed of nineteen major constituent companies and numerous minor sub-constituent ones. Some of those nineteen had previously taken over some minor companies themselves in the years prior to Grouping. Although the number of companies absorbed into the LMS was far fewer than with the GWR, those companies that were formed some of the biggest in the country, making the LMS the largest company out of the Big Four.

The Midland Railway was the largest company to become part of the LMS, followed closely by the London & North Western Railway (which had amalgamated with the Lancashire & Yorkshire Railway in 1922), the Caledonian Railway, the Highland Railway and the North London Railway. The passenger-carrying bodies of at least eight of those absorbed companies are currently known to exist today in various conditions.

The Lancashire & Yorkshire Railway was incorporated in 1847 from an amalgamation of several companies. From then until 1923, it was the third largest company operating in Northern England (the other two being the Midland and the North Eastern railways).

Built in 1913, this 60-foot, ten-compartment, third-class L&YR bogie was No. 3290 (later LMS No. 13814 in 1923 and No. 15242 in 1933). Withdrawn from service in 1952, it was purchased and transferred to a remote farm in Rathen, Aberdeenshire, where it was to be used as a function room for family and special occasions, as well as for meetings. During the mid-1990s it became unsafe to house these occasions and was then used as a general store. By the time I visited, on 27 March 2016, it had not been used for many years and was in a derelict condition, as can be clearly seen.

The London & North Western Railway was formed in 1846 with the amalgamation of the Grand Junction, London & Birmingham and Manchester & Birmingham railways. Its headquarters were at Euston station in London and it had approximately 350 miles of track.

This vehicle, numbered 2955, was one of a batch of thirty-eight built between 1914 and 1917. Like many other L&NWR coaches, this vehicle was put into service with the ambulance trains of the First World War, becoming a pharmacy car. It was sold as surplus stock after the war in the early 1920s, at which point it was taken to the middle of a field at Ryton in Herefordshire to be used as a stable for the ponies of a local riding school. It was here that I photographed it on 7 June 1997, when it had been out of use for about ten years prior to my visit. I was informed by the owner that he wanted to get rid of the body, but was reluctant to scrap it as he would like to see it preserved. He was therefore offering it free to anybody who might want it. Following on from an extensive advertising campaign in newspapers and railway magazines, as well as contacting various preservation societies/museums, by 2004 there were no takers for his offer, so he was left with no option but to break it up where it had stood for about eighty years.

Midland Railway six-wheeled, five-compartment, third-class carriage No. 355 was built at Derby in 1890. It was purchased second-hand by the Brecon & Merthyr Railway in 1920 and became part of the GWR in 1923. Following its withdrawal in 1925, the body ended up as a café on the A30 in Devon, before being transported to the garden of a house near Wedmore, Somerset, sometime during the 1980s, where it was used as a garden shed. I took this picture of it there on 16 July 2005; however, two years later it was moved to the Somerset & Dorset Railway Heritage Trust premises in Midsomer Norton. A couple of years later it was mounted onto the underframe of a London, Midland & Scottish Railway covered carriage truck vehicle (whose body was subsequently scrapped). It is currently undergoing major restoration.

The Midland Railway originated in 1832 and was built with the purpose of serving the coal trade in the Leicestershire and Nottinghamshire areas. In 1844 and 1846 it was merged with four other companies, which at the time made it the third largest railway operator in the country.

Built in 1907 for the MR at Derby, No. 349 was one of two six-wheeled clerestory-roofed picnic saloons. Following its withdrawal from service during the mid-1930s, the body was sold and taken to Mackworth in Derbyshire, where it was used as a storage shed and workshop, and was pictured as such on 25 May 2003. By 2005 this vehicle had been recovered by the Midland Railway Centre Trust, based at Butterley in Derbyshire, where it has been mounted onto a LMS bogie bolster freight wagon underframe. It is currently one of the many projects that is awaiting restoration in order to join the vintage vehicles that are housed in the trust's museum at Swanwick Junction.

The Manchester South Junction & Altrincham Railway (MSJ&AR) came into being in 1845 and operated an 8.5-mile route between Altrincham in Cheshire and London Road station in Manchester (which is now Manchester Piccadilly). It subsequently became part of the LMS at Grouping in 1923. It has achieved some status of notoriety in that it is one of the few suburban railways that can boast of operating three different systems of electrification. The first of these came in the late 1920s/early 1930s with the introduction of the 1,500 V DC overhead system. This was changed during the 1950s and '60s to the British Railways standard 25 kV AC overhead system, and in 1992 the southern end of the line became part of the 750 V AC Manchester Metrolink light rail system, and remains so to this day.

Little information regarding the stock of the MSJ&AR is available, and very few examples are known to survive. These remaining two compartments from carriage No. 02467 are believed to have been built in around 1873 at Wolverton works in Buckinghamshire. After having been being moved from a nearby location, where they were previously used as a garden shed. They were photographed here in use as an office and information centre in a community orchard in Wolverton on 14 August 2010.

Companies Amalgamated into the London & North Eastern Railway (LNER)

Out of the Big Four, the London & North Eastern Railway was the second largest behind the LMS. Formed of eleven major constituent companies, it also co-owned and ran twenty-one smaller companies along with the LMS. Among those constituent companies, the largest ones were the Great Eastern, Great Central, Great Northern, North British, North Eastern and the Great North of Scotland railways. The LNER also co-owned the Midland & Great North Joint Railway with the LMS, which was the biggest joint-owned railway in the country.

Bodies from nine out of the eleven constituent companies can be found dotted all across the country. The other two companies had no rolling stock of their own, and instead leased units from two of the other nine companies in order to operate.

Constructed at the Great Eastern Railway's Stratford works in the East End of London in 1887, No. 203 was built as a six-wheeled, four-compartment, first and second-class luggage composite. It was not re-numbered into the LNER numbering scheme and was withdrawn in 1928, when it was sold (along with a sister GER vehicle). The two were taken to Whittlesey Road in Peterborough, Cambridgeshire, where they were put side-by-side and were turned into a residence. It was photographed still being used as such on 16 February 2013, some seventy-five years after having been withdrawn and converted.

This carriage, No. 1085, has led a varied, somewhat charmed life. It was built by the GER at Stratford in 1887 as a six-wheeled, six-compartment, third-class carriage. Later, under the ownership of the LNER, it was re-numbered to 60741. Following its withdrawal in 1935, the body was sold to a farmer in Boston, Lincolnshire, where it was used as a chicken coop. In 1982 it was rescued and taken to the Rutland Railway Museum in Cottesmore, Leicestershire, where it was left in the open, awaiting restoration. However, this never materialised (with only a cosmetic 'touch-up' of the bodywork taking place). After twenty years of being left to the elements, it was purchased in 2002 by the owner of the Trading Post (a farm shop that specialises in fresh organic and locally produced foods) in Lopen, Somerset. Transferred to the owner's site, it was placed on a suitable hard standing and used as a tea room and café, as shown in this photograph, taken on 24 June 2007.

The Great Northern Railway was formed in 1846 and ran between King's Cross in London and York, via Peterborough and Grantham. This clerestory-roofed vehicle was built as No. 1002 in 1902 at the railway's works in Doncaster, South Yorkshire. During the same year that it came under the ownership of the LNER (1923) it was involved in a shunting accident at Heck on the Selby to Doncaster line, wherein it knocked four wagons through the buffer stops, which overturned. Riding along on the wheels of those upturned wagons, it mounted the roof of a nearby house, where it came to an abrupt stop. Fortunately, it was soon repaired and put back into service, lasting for another twenty-three years, until its withdrawal in 1946.

Its body was sold and moved to an address in York, where it had to be shortened slightly in order to fit into the owner's back garden, with the hope it would be used to house a railwayana museum. However, this did not materialise, and it was used as a garden shed/workshop instead. I visited the location on 17 July 2012 and it was still being used as such. It is believed that it has now been sold and moved to an as yet undisclosed location, where it will possibly be restored to its former glory.

The North Eastern Railway was formed in 1854. Following the incorporation of seventeen existing railway companies, it was then amalgamated into the LNER. Unlike many of the other pre-Grouping companies, its operating territory was a relatively small and compact one. This vehicle, No. 1644, was built at the company's works in York around 1866 and is a six-wheeled, five-compartment, first/third-class composite. Following its withdrawal in the 1930s, the body was acquired and transported to the idyllic setting of Thorpe Underwood for use as holiday accommodation beside the Ouse Gill Beck Lake (which is an offshoot of the River Ouse). It is pictured at this location on 6 April 2012, with the lake in the background. By October 2014, however, it had been acquired by the Tanfield Railway Preservation Society in Wearside and placed on an underframe, where it is currently awaiting restoration.

Companies Amalgamated into the Southern Railway (SR)

The Southern Railway was formed from ten major constituent companies (the largest of these being the London & South Western, the London, Brighton & South Coast and the South Eastern & Chatham railways), but it also ran over twenty smaller railways that were formerly owned by some of the major constituents, but were not big enough to be deemed constituents themselves. They also ran and co-owned the highly popular Somerset & Dorset Joint Railway with the LMS. Another railway that came under the auspices of the SR was the Lynton & Barnstaple Railway. Being narrow gauge, it was not covered under the Railways Act of 1921.

The SR inherited numerous carriages from its constituent companies, with the largest proportion of these being Victorian-built wooden-bodied examples. The various works, depots and yards operated by the Southern Railway saw surplus bodies becoming grounded and used as staff canteens, mess rooms and engineers' stores. The bodies of the passenger vehicles of at least eight of those constituent companies can still be found, with a large quantity having been dotted along the South Coast, where they are used as bungalows and summer houses.

Formed in 1846 by the amalgamation of five other companies, the London, Brighton & South Coast Railway formed a triangle of lines. With London at its apex, it took in the whole of the Sussex coastline at its base, with parts of Surrey and Kent forming its sides. It was bordered on the west of the country by the London & South Western Railway and by the SER/SE&CR on its eastern side. It became part of the Southern Railway at Grouping in 1923.

Built in 1893 at the railway's Brighton works, No. 106 was a six-wheeled, four-compartment, first-class carriage. It was re-numbered 7527 by the Southern Railway in 1923 (this number is still carried on the inside of two doors), and was withdrawn from service in late 1929. In early 1930 the body was purchased from the works at Brighton and was placed onto a road trailer, being towed 15 miles to its new home at Oxbottom, near Newick, for use as a summer house. When photographed at that location on 4 August 2012, it was still on the same road trailer it had been transported there on eighty-two years earlier, although by now it had become a storage shed.

In some cases you cannot immediately see that there is anything unusual about a property, and would probably never think that it contained a railway carriage, as is the case with this example seen at Pagham on 19 May 2018. Although it doesn't look like it, this house actually contains two railway carriages, placed side-by-side. These can be discerned by the two curved shapes that are visible at the top of the building, just below the roof line. This property is different in that the carriages are placed immediately next to each other, with no gap in between, and with a flat roof placed over the top of them, instead of an apex roof. They are probably of LB&SCR origin, as the vast majority of vehicles found in this seaside hamlet seem to be.

Another location on the South Coast that was well-known for its houses made out of railway carriages was Shoreham-by-Sea. There was one particular area, known locally as 'Bungalow Town', that consisted of about ninety homes built around railway carriage bodies, along similar lines to those at Pagham along the coast. The area became very popular with actors and actresses appearing in shows at theatres along the South Coast and it was affectionately referred to by locals as 'the Los Angeles of the South of England'.

In recognition of this nickname, most of the houses were named after characters found in pantomimes and stage plays. On the occasion of my visit on 19 May 2018, there were only two properties that still retained both of their railway carriage bodies. this location was originally named 'Cinderella' (although it didn't appear to have the name on it) and this particular example was built in 1881 by the LB&SCR at their Brighton works as a four-compartment, first/second class composite vehicle and was given the number 364.

The London, Chatham & Dover Railway formed a significant part of the London commuter network. The company went bankrupt in 1867, mainly due to the competition and duplication of services offered by the South Eastern Railway, but was somehow able to continue to operate. In 1898 both companies agreed to run the two railways as a single company and the South Eastern & Chatham Railway was formed. This was not an amalgamation, however, as both companies remained separate and kept their own shareholders.

Built at the LC&DR works at Longhedge in Battersea, London, in 1897 this was a six-wheeled, five-compartment, third-class coach (which was converted to a brake third in 1910). It began life as No. 668 and was transferred to the newly formed SE&CR in 1907, where it was re-numbered 3188. At Grouping in 1923, it came under the ownership of the Southern Railway and was re-numbered again to 3652. It was withdrawn in 1935 and along with a London & South Western Railway carriage body was taken to Yarcombe in Devon, where the two were placed side-by-side as a bungalow. At the time of my visit on 8 October 1996, the other vehicle could not be seen from the outside; however, this one could be seen from the rear of the property. Following the passing away of the owner, in 2005 both bodies were rescued by the Bluebell Railway, after some seventy years of being used as a family home.

In 1838 the London & Southampton Railway was formed in order to link the capital to the port at Southampton, which has been an important port for trade since the days of the Romans and was during the Victorian era the third most popular port in the country (behind London and Bristol), to be associated with cruises. In 1840 the railway changed its name to the London & South Western Railway, following its extended and growing network of lines, which included those going from London to Plymouth via Salisbury and Exeter (to offer a different route from that of the GWR), and its branches stretched to Ilfracombe and Padstow on the North Devon and Cornwall coastlines respectively.

This vehicle was built at the company's Nine Elms carriage and locomotive works in London in 1890. Numbered 903, it was a six-wheeled, five-compartment, third-class coach. Later, just before the outbreak of the First World War, it was re-numbered 705 in the L&SWR's re-numbering scheme. It was sold upon its withdrawal from service in 1922 and, like numerous other vehicles, ended up as holiday accommodation and homes at Selsey in Sussex, on the South Coast. It was photographed there by myself on 10 January 2004. Despite having been considerably modernised and extended, it was still recognisable as a railway carriage.

1836 saw the formation of the South Eastern Railway, which had incorporated the London & Greenwich and the Canterbury & Whitstable railways among others. It was the main competitor of the L&CDR until 1898, when the two companies semi-merged to form the SE&CR (as described earlier in this chapter).

Vehicles that originate from this railway are very rare now, although some recent examples have been found upon being bequeathed to the Bluebell Railway due the passing of the people who were living in them. This example is believed to have been built in the late 1870s as a four-wheeled, five-compartment, third-class vehicle. Its original number (or any others) is presently unknown. It was withdrawn from service in 1928 and was transferred – along with five other bodies – to the tiny East Sussex village of Rye Harbour, where it was used as a tea room, and later that year as a makeshift hospital/headquarters following the capsizing of the lifeboat *Mary Stanford*. When I visited the site on 30 December 2007, it was being used as a holiday home.

The Somerset & Dorset Railway was formed in 1862 when the Somerset and Dorset Central Railways amalgamated to become a single company. It was unique in that it fell under the joint ownership of the London & South Western and Midland Railways; it was agreed between the two of them that the Midland would provide and maintain the locomotives and motive power while the LSWR would be responsible for the carriage and wagon rolling stock and for the upkeep and maintenance of the infrastructure. In 1923, at the grouping, it was re-named the Somerset & Dorset Joint Railway and came under the joint ownership of the newly formed LMS and Southern Railways and the same pre-grouping proviso would still exist. The line was closed in 1966 as part of the infamous Doctor Beeching railway closures.

Vehicles from this railway are very hard to come by. This example was built by Cravens at Sheffield in 1891 as a six-wheeled, five-compartment third class and numbered 68 and was transferred to the Southern Railway in 1923 (its SR number is not currently known) before being finally withdrawn in October 1932. The body was purchased from the works at Highbridge by members of the Mark Tennis Club and used by them as a clubhouse/pavilion; in the early 1960s the club had decided to build a brand new clubhouse and the body was sold to the father of a member who used it on his farm nearby as a lambing shed until 1976. It was then purchased by the current owner and taken to his home in Somerset. However, due to space restrictions one end was removed and two compartments were 'flat-packed' for storage; the end was then re-attached, forming the partial body seen here on 8 April 2018, where it is used as a reading room. Several components from the two removed compartments were later donated to the Somerset & Dorset Trust at Washford and were used as part of the restoration of another S&DJR carriage (*see Chapter 19*).

CHAPTER 2

Post-Grouping Passenger Carriages

Great Western Railway (GWR)

Although the GWR inherited the largest number of constituent companies at Grouping, the majority of them had scarcely any rolling stock. While some of its constituent companies' stock can still be found, the vast majority of GWR stock is actually from the original company itself, prior to Grouping taking place.

This vehicle was built in 1880 as a four-wheeled, four-compartment, third-class carriage. Numbered 224, it was re-numbered 6723 at Grouping and was withdrawn in 1930. Upon its withdrawal, the body became a house at Greensplat in Cornwall. At the time of my visit on 9 May 1997, one end of the body was all that remained intact, due to the house being demolished in 1995 (except for the chimney breast, which was still in situ). However, if you try to visit Greensplat today, you will not find it, because in 2000 the nearby English China Clay quarry expanded its operations and the entire village was completely demolished.

The GWR was unique from the other companies in relation to the numbering of its carriages; apart from having the number painted on the outside as standard, they also stamped the number into every door frame on the hinged side, and this was especially true with the wooden-bodied vehicles. However, the number was not just stamped once on the door frame, but was usually repeated in three or four places on the same side. Like some other companies from the pre-Grouping era, the GWR etched the company initials, 'GWR' or 'GWR Swindon', into the brass door handles. Taking this further than most other companies, the company also etched the door hinges and window latches in the same way.

The GWR numbered its stock into numerical order, and in some instances old numbers would be re-used where there was a gap in the series. For example, an original GWR vehicle, numbered 123, may have been scrapped or destroyed in an accident or war, and so to replace the one lost the company would renumber a vehicle acquired at Grouping as No. 123.

The majority of bodies that can be found that came from the Great Western Railway in actual fact came from the original GWR, so the vehicles featured in this chapter were all built prior to 1923.

This vehicle was built at Swindon works in 1888 as a four-wheeled, four-compartment, first-class unit. It was converted to a first/second-class composite vehicle (having two first and two second-class compartments) in 1898, for suburban London services – hence the rounded tops visible above the doors. In 1914 it was transferred for use on the Whitland to Pembroke line in South Wales and was re-numbered 139. Following Grouping, the GWR re-numbered it again to 6139. It was withdrawn quite late for an original GWR vehicle, in 1938, and the body was purchased and taken to the Innis Downs roundabout at Lanivet, near Bodmin, where it was used as a fully functional addition to a bungalow (complete with fireplace and chimney). It was photographed still being used as such on 19 June 2011.

Nestled in a little cove at Llangrannog in Ceredigion in Wales is this Swindon-built, five-compartment, first/second-class luggage clerestory-roofed composite, dating from 1876. It is in use as a holiday home that is rented out. Originally numbered 282, it was built as an eight-wheeled broad gauge vehicle that was converted when the GWR was forced to change to standard gauge in 1854, when it was re-numbered 965, before finally becoming No. 6965 in 1923. It was withdrawn in 1930 and transported (with some difficulty, it must be assumed, since the roads that led down to it were very narrow and twisting in places) to the spot where it was pictured on 25 May 2002.

At Cockshute Garden in Newport can be found the bodies of two GWR 1884-built, six-wheeled, five-compartment, third-class carriages, Nos 1558 and 1620, which had been withdrawn in 1931. Placed side by side and with an apex roof constructed over the pair, these bodies became a house on a smallholding and were used as such until the late 1960s. Seen here on 24 August 2012 is the front of these two – namely, No. 1620. Despite not having been lived in for over thirty years, it is still in a fairly good condition when seen (as is the other vehicle). They were used in later years as storage sheds for plant pot trays, the type that are found in garden centres and nurseries.

Following withdrawal from service, in 1933 the bodies of two GWR clerestory-roofed, non-corridor, seven-compartment, third-class carriages (Nos 1800 and 1813) were purchased and transported to Market Lavington in Wiltshire. Once there they were placed side-by-side and a tall apex roof was added over the top of them, to make a very luxurious bungalow. On 19 July 1997 I visited the property and was invited in for tea and cake while the elderly couple who lived there related the story of the day the carriages arrived and were craned into place. In 2007 the bodies were at risk of being demolished by the new owners of the property, who had applied for planning permission to build a four-bedroom house on the site. Thankfully, this application was declined, and so the carriages can continue to be enjoyed as a family home hopefully for many more years to come. The vehicle shown in the picture is the rear of the property and is No. 1813.

This vehicle, No. 283, was built in 1897 as a first-class saloon at Swindon works and was used as part of Queen Victoria's Diamond Jubilee Royal Train, in which the queen's ladies-in-waiting travelled. It was re-numbered 8283 in 1909 and was used as part of the Jubilee train until 1925. Withdrawal came in 1932 and in 1933 a group of residents from the village of Shirwell, in North Devon, got together to purchase the body. It was towed from nearby Barnstaple station by a company from Umberleigh using a steam traction engine and was taken to the north-west corner of a field on the outskirts of the village, where corrugated sheeting was affixed to three of its sides and the roof. The remains of the interior compartments were removed and a wooden skittle alley was built onto the floor. The remaining fourth side was covered by a hedgerow and, on my visit there on 6 November 1999, this hedgerow continued to act as a shield against the elements. This side is in original condition. The skittle club closed in 2014, and by August 2015 the body/alley had been declared by Historic England as having Grade II listed status, which means it will survive for many more years. At the time of writing, no decision has been made as to what the body will be used for next.

London, Midland & Scottish Railway (LMS)

The largest company of the Big Four was the LMS. Unlike the GWR, this was a new company formed at the amalgamation in 1923, and at that time it found itself in possession of 20,276 carriages. As well as including part of Ireland under its jurisdiction, the LMS also owned numerous canals, docks and harbours that had been acquired from former companies during Grouping.

The LMS was not as meticulous in the numbering of its stock as the GWR was. While the railway did stamp the numbers of the vehicles into the bodywork, the markings were not so numerous, usually appearing once on each door, principally in the wooden slatted area behind the louvres, above the doors. Considering the amount of carriages the LMS owned, this would have been a thankless, never-ending task, especially when you take into account the company's re-numbering programme in 1933. Due to the LMS having scrapped the vast majority of its pre-Grouping stock, this endeavour was undertaken to bring their records up to date.

Many LMS passenger carriages were sold to preservation societies as complete carriages and can be found in museums and on heritage railways to this day, but there were a still a fair few that ended up as grounded bodies and which still exist as such.

This nine-compartment, third-class bogie was built by the LMSR at their works in Wolverton, Buckinghamshire, in 1937 as their No. 11987. Following its withdrawal from service by British Railways in the early 1960s, the body was taken to a remote farm in Corgarff, Aberdeenshire, where it was used as a stable for horses originally, before becoming a home for sheep, goats and geese. In later years it became used as a general store shed, which was how it was photographed by myself on 2 August 2004. Sadly, by late 2013 its condition had deteriorated quite badly, and it was therefore scrapped on site by November of that year.

23

Built at Wolverton in 1934 and numbered 20780, this vehicle began life as a five-compartment brake third bogie. It was withdrawn from service in the mid-1950s and the body was sold to a farmer in Kirton of Tough in Aberdeenshire. Upon arrival at the farm it was placed in front of the farmhouse to be used as a general storage shed. However, it was too long and one end obscured the entrance of the farmhouse, so it was decided to remove two compartments from one end and use the remainder as a garage, which is how it was still being used at the time of my visit on 26 March 2013; indeed, the rear of the current family car can be made out through the window panel on the right. Due to the ground eroding away over the years and leaving the body in a precarious position, the owner only uses the right-hand end, with the family car being placed just inside to protect it from the elements. The body is prevented from falling over as it is securely tied to the metal post on the right of the picture by several webbed lifting slings. The other two compartments are still on site, on the opposite side of the yard, and are used as a general storage shed.

This unidentified nine-compartment, third-class carriage was probably built during the 1930s. It was purchased in early 1963, so it can be assumed that it was withdrawn sometime in 1962. For a few years it was left outside to the elements, but it was lived in by a family of six people while their home was being constructed by the father and his three brothers. Later it became used as a log and furniture storage shed. At the time of my visit to the location in Mosshead, Aberdeenshire, on 3 August 2004, a purpose-built shed was being constructed around the body, which was going to become a workshop, complete with lathes and other machinery. The first three compartments will be left outside of the building, with one end removed and double doors fitted in order to continue being used as a wood store. However, in order to make this possible, a small gap will be have to be cut between the compartments in the area where the lining on the roof changes colour. This gap will be big enough to accommodate the shed front and the door, which will be made from corrugated metal sheets.

London & North Eastern Railway (LNER)

The LNER also owned some canals and numerous shipping vessels that were acquired in 1923, when it was formed. The company was similar to the LMS in regards to numbering its wooden vehicles, in that it stamped them in the same place as the LMS units, although one of the companies that was absorbed into the LNER (the Great Eastern Railway) stamped the numbers of the vehicles into the wooden solebar on each end near the buffers. One thing the LNER did do, however, was add a digit to the front of the existing number depending on which company they had previously belonged to. For example, if a carriage was originally built for the Great Eastern Railway and was numbered 228, then its new number under the LNER would be 5228.

In 1930 the LNER underwent a re-numbering of all its stock. At the time of the amalgamation the railway owned 20,000 carriages, so this re-numbering would remove those vehicles from the company's books. This was a practice that the LMS would also undertake three years later, as previously mentioned.

There have been instances where a body has been discovered on a farm, for example, bearing the LNER livery and its number on the outside of the body, as well as the stamped number on the solebar or somewhere on the inside. This practice of stamping the vehicle internally having hailed from pre-Grouping companies, this identifies the body as not having been built by the LNER, but by one of the companies it had absorbed.

When built in 1924 at the LNER works in York, this particular bogie vehicle would have been 61.5 feet in length and was classified as a seven and a half-compartment, locker composite corridor carriage (with the locker forming the half compartment). The configuration was two first-class and five second-class compartments. The year this vehicle was built saw the introduction of a new numbering system, with all LNER carriages being numbered in their own series from 10000 upwards and a suffix letter being applied that would denote the section/area those vehicles were allocated to work. This example was number 10168J, with the letter J denoting that this vehicle would work on the East Coast. Upon its withdrawal in the 1950s, the body was taken to a clifftop at Crawton, near Stonehaven in Aberdeenshire, where it was cut into two halves and used as two summer houses. One half deteriorated quite rapidly over the years and was scrapped during the 1980s. The other half was still being used as a summer house when I visited on 3 August 2004. Sadly, this also became a victim of exposure to the sea air and deteriorated beyond use, being finally scrapped by 2010.

This corridor third-class vehicle was built by the Birmingham Railway Carriage & Wagon Company in 1936 as a batch of forty-six for the LNER. It was withdrawn after the end of steam services in 1968, when its body was purchased and taken by road to Bograxie Croft in Kemnay, Aberdeenshire, where it was used as a general storage shed. It was still at this location on 25 March 2016, albeit being in a semi-derelict condition. Parts from this vehicle have been used by the LNER Carriage Association to restore other vehicles in their collection to running order, so it is highly unlikely that this body will be saved, as it will more than likely collapse if moved. Note how the owner had the good sense to mount the body on what can be described as a small purpose-built stone wall-like base, which has prevented the floor from rotting out over the years.

Southern Railway (SR)

Despite inheriting several carriages at Grouping, SR-built carriages are mainly found as complete vehicles in museums and on preservation sites. This makes the bodies of SR passenger-carrying vehicles quite a rare find; in fact, in the twenty-three years that I have been studying and recording these vehicles, I have not seen or photographed a single passenger carriage that was built by the SR after 1923 that has been used for another purpose. There are, however, plenty of pre-Grouping companies' vehicles around.

CHAPTER 3

Pullman Carriages

The Pullman Palace Car Company was the brainchild of twenty-two-year-old American businessman George Mortimer Pullman, who, on his honeymoon in around 1855, travelled with his new bride for 58 miles from Buffalo in New York State to Westfield in Massachusetts in a sleeping car (which had been introduced on American railroads some twenty years earlier). It was a very uncomfortable journey and a dissatisfied George spent the majority of the night and the following weeks trying to come up with ideas for how to make the journey more comfortable, thus making it a more enjoyable ride for the passengers.

Although he tried to sell his idea to various railroad companies, they all declined to back him citing the reason that the idea was an uneconomic one. Undeterred despite these knockbacks, Pullman purchased a day coach from the Chicago & Alton (C&A) Railroad and teamed up with Leonard Seibert, who was a skilled cabinetmaker from Chicago, and together they proceeded to convert the vehicle into a sleeping car, utilising Pullman's idea of making the vehicle more comfortable to ride in. Eventually the C&A finally agreed, after much persuading from George, to include the car in one of their trains, and in 1859 it ran the 120 miles from Bloomington to Chicago as part of the consist. It proved to be moderately successful, however, and the biggest problem was encountered when the conductor on the train tried to get the male passengers to remove their boots prior to getting into the bunks as they were rather reluctant to do so.

Pullman converted a further eleven cars and was operating a small fleet of a dozen – but only on lines not designated as being 'main-line'. Despite this small success the C&A (one of the largest rail companies in America at that time) still refused to financially back the venture. George, being the entrepreneur that he was, saw the perfect opportunity to raise the money that he required. During the height of the now famous Pike's Peak Gold Rush in Colorado, he moved to a Colorado mining town and opened a trading store selling supplies to the prospectors. With the money that he made, he returned to Chicago and built his own first railway car from scratch, which he named *Pioneer*. The vehicle was immaculate and opulent to look at and was greatly admired by all who saw it. However, there was one main stumbling block which he had not reckoned on, which was that it was out of gauge with the platforms and bridges along the C&A route. Having spent all of his money on the project, he was ready to turn his back on the whole idea and seek his fortunes elsewhere, but Lady Luck continued to smile upon him. In 1865, as the train that was carrying the body of the assassinated President Abraham Lincoln from Washington DC to Springfield, Illinois, reached Chicago, Mrs Lincoln collapsed due to exhaustion. This was attributed to several factors, one of which was that the train stopped at every station along the way in order for the population to pay their respects, and memorial services were held at each stop. George seized the opportunity and offered the lady the use of his car to take her directly to Chicago without having to make further stops along the way. The C&A had no choice but to accept his offer and a sizeable army of navvies was dispatched and set to work altering the platforms and bridges between Chicago and Springfield in order to accommodate the car.

Sometime later, one of Lincoln's successors, General Ulysses S. Grant, spent an overnight journey in Pullman's car and declared it was the most comfortable and pleasant ride that he had ever experienced in any railroad car. With such a resounding endorsement the railroad companies almost fell over each other in their attempts to acquire Pullman vehicles, and the funds needed to build them became readily available. So, in 1867 at the young age of thirty-six, George was the owner and founder of the Pullman Palace & Car Company in Detroit, Michigan, and the first contract of business naturally went to the Chicago & Alton Railroad, and the name of Pullman became synonymous with luxury premier rail travel and is still to this day, some 151 years on.

Historically, this vehicle is one of the most important vehicles to be preserved: it was the first Pullman carriage ordered by the Midland Railway. It was built as a sleeping car at the Detroit workshops of the Pullman Palace & Car Company in 1873 and was given the name *Midland*. At the end of the year it was 'flat-packed' and shipped across the Atlantic to Derby – it was deemed that this was the safest way to transport these vehicles. It was re-assembled at Derby in January 1874 and entered service in June of that year, although this was for one week only; it was then withdrawn and sent across the English Channel to Paris so that the general manager of the Pullman office could use it on an extensive tour of Europe in order to promote the company. It returned to England in 1877 and was re-built as a day car. In 1879 it was loaned to the Great Northern Railway for use on their east coast line between April and June of that year. The name was removed in 1883 and it was re-numbered to No. 21 in 1888; it carried this number until finally being withdrawn from service just after the First World War due to a decline in the use of Pullman Cars. Following this, the body was grounded near to Skipton station in Yorkshire where it was used as a mess room/stores and office by the local carriage & wagon department. In 1970 Derby museums enquired about purchasing the body, which was offered to them for £65; due to financial difficulties in raising the capital it was not actually acquired by them until 1972 and it would be a further two years before the body was moved from site. The first place it was taken to was the former barracks of the Sherwood Foresters at Normanton in Derbyshire before being transferred to the ownership of the Midland Railway Trust and taken from the barracks to their centre at Butterley in 1981, where it was placed onto the disused platform there. Upon visiting the centre on 10 April 1994, it was still sat on the platform. However, a visit these days will find the body inside the on-site Matthew Kirtley museum building, on the underframe of an LMSR carriage.

In 1872, the disgruntled General Manager of the Midland Railway visited America and saw first-hand the travelling experience that passengers were enjoying on the George Pullman vehicles. As a result, he discussed the option of using Pullman cars with the Midland Traffic Committee, and in 1873 it was agreed that Pullman would supply the cars, with the allowance that he would supply his own attendants and have permission to charge his own supplement on top of any fares. This agreement would last for a period of fifteen years, but the Midland also added the proviso that Pullman would also build carriages with the same design for all three classes of passenger, and that baggage/brake cars would also be built.

This vehicle was one of four baggage cars, numbered 1–4, that were shipped in 'flat-pack' form from Detroit to Derby in 1873 and were then re-assembled and entered into service with the Midland Railway in 1874. These cars proved to be very unpopular with the general public, but the MR persisted with them in service until 1888, which was the period agreed on with the Pullman company. They then were withdrawn from revenue-earning service and transferred to the departmental fleet. In 1972 this vehicle (which one of the four is its actual identity is presently unknown) and another vehicle (a first/second class composite) were purchased by the Midland Railway project – now the Midland Railway Trust – for £69 each and in 1975 they were removed from Bradford Forster Square, where they had been used as staff mess rooms and canteens, and taken to Butterley. Sadly, the composite vehicle was destroyed in an arson attack in 2012 but this example, seen here on 12 January 2008, still remains in situ.

It wasn't only the Midland Railway that benefitted from the advantages of Pullman cars built in America and shipped to the UK for re-assembling. From 1915 onwards, every Pullman car was allocated a schedule number (irrespective of which company would be owning them). This was in addition to any name or running number.

Built in 1891 by the Gilbert Car Manufacturing Co. in New York for the South Eastern Railway for use in their 'Hastings Car Train', this vehicle was re-assembled at Ashford works in Kent. Its schedule number was 103 and it was named *Dolphin*. Five years later, in 1896, it was rebuilt in order to enclose the vestibules and end corridor connections. In 1920 it was rebuilt again as a parlour car at Longhedge works by the Pullman Company, before finally being withdrawn in 1930.

It can now be found at Selsey in Sussex, where, along with many other carriage bodies, it is in use as a holiday home. At the time of my visit there on 10 January 2004, the house it was part of was in the process of having extension work done to it. The carriage can barely be seen nowadays from the outside as the result of that work.

Another SER vehicle that became a parlour car was this example. It was built in 1897 by the Metropolitan Carriage & Wagon Company as a first-class car for the SER's 'Folkstone Vestibule Ltd'. It was schedule number 86 and carried the name *Mabel*. In 1919 it was rebuilt again by the Pullman Company at Longhedge works and continued to carry passengers up until 1930, when it was withdrawn. Just like the previous image, this vehicle also ended up at Selsey, in use as a holiday home, and was pictured as such on 10 January 2004.

Being given the schedule number of 22 and named *Princess Ena*, this Pullman kitchen car vehicle was built in 1906 for the London, Brighton & South Coast Railway. It was one of the three last vehicles that were built in America for use in this country. It was withdrawn in 1932 and was moved to Selsey in Sussex and became this rather splendid-looking house. The photograph was taken on 10 January 2004.

CHAPTER 4

Irish Railways Passenger Carriages

Railways in Ireland can be traced back to 1826, with a railway between Limerick & Waterford being given authorisation to operate (although for some reason this did not proceed). The first to be built and operated, however, came in 1834, with the building of the 6-mile-long Dublin & Kingstown Railway. Just like on the mainland, services in Ireland were originally operated by a number of different railway companies. However, at the turn of the twentieth century the mainline railways of Ireland had been grouped into eight railways, although there were also some twenty-five minor independent railways also operating. There was also the unique Listowel & Ballybunion Railway, which was the world's first commercial monorail.

There were three main railway companies that operated in Northern Ireland: the Great Northern Railway of Ireland (GNRI), the Belfast & County Down Railway (B&CDR) and the Northern Counties Committee (NCC), which came under the ownership of the Midland Railway and subsequently the LMS after the grouping on the mainland in 1923. In January 1948 the railways were nationalised both on the mainland and in Northern Ireland. In Ireland the Transport Act (Northern Ireland) created the Ulster Transport Authority (UTA), which was responsible for the running of all public transport, which included the B&CDR. A year later the NCC came under their ownership and finally, in 1958, the GNRI was also taken over by the UTA. In 1967 the UTA was split into two operations – Northern Ireland Railways would operate and maintain rail services, while the road traffic would continue to be operated and maintained by the UTA.

There were four main railway companies operating in the Irish Free State (later to become known as Eire or the Republic of Ireland). They were: the Midland Great Western, the Southern & Western, the Dublin & South Eastern and the Cork, Bandon & South Coast, and in 1924 they all decided to join together and form one company, the Great Southern Railway (GSR). The Transport Act of 1944 saw the GSR become a private company and from 1945 onwards it has been known as Coras Iompair Eireann (CIE). The company also took control of the Dublin United Transport Company (DUTC), which had been responsible for operating trams and buses in the Dublin area. Since 1986 the CIE has been operating the three largest internal transport companies in the republic – Bus Eireann, Dublin Bus and Irish Rail, along with its offshoot the Dublin Area Rapid Transit (DART) system.

The first three railways to operate in Ireland all had different gauges for their tracks. The Dublin & Kingstown Railway shared the same gauge as the UK – 4 feet 8.5 inches; the Dublin & Drogheda Railway had a gauge of 5 feet 2 inches; and the Ulster Railway was 6 feet 2 inches. The Board of Trade (who were responsible for all decisions regarding commerce and industry in Ireland) received several complaints from the Ulster Railway regarding the difference in gauge sizes and upon investigating they decided that from 1843 the standard gauge for the country's railways would be set at 5 feet 3 inches and it remains so to this day. The Ulster Railway was compensated far more than the others, due to having to re-gauge its stock to a greater difference. During the 1950s and 1960s the railways were heavily rationalised (much like the Beeching cuts in the UK) and many miles of lines were lost. One of the biggest of these was the closure of the entire rail network in West Cork, leaving some 130 miles between Mullingar & Derry with no rail network at all, which had a devastating effect on the economy in that part of the country, which relied on tourism.

Although there aren't as many passenger carriage bodies in Ireland as on the mainland, there are still some interesting examples dotted about.

Opening on 1 March 1888 and running the 10 miles between Listowel and Ballybunion in County Kerry, the Listowel to Ballybunion Railway was more commonly known as the Lartigue Monorailway, named after French Engineer Charles Lartigue. The railway was not a monorail in the truest sense of the meaning as it had two horizontal rails fitted about halfway down each side, which did not carry any weight, but unpowered stabilising rails were fitted onto all the engines, coaches and wagons, which would come into contact with the rails to prevent the vehicles from overbalancing.

As well as carrying passengers, the railway was also used by a number of farmers as a way of taking their livestock to market. Livestock would be strategically placed in the carriage in order to balance the train out. For example, on one side of the wagon there would be a full grown cow, while two calves would be positioned on the other side. Later in the day, the train might be spotted again with the two calves in each half of the wagon. As the farmer may have wanted to sell the cow at market, the two calves had to go along to balance it, and they would balance each other on the return. The same principle applied to the passengers; they were arrayed in the carriages in such a way as to try and make each side balance the other out and they could not move while the train was in motion. During the Irish Civil War between 1921 and 1923 the railway sustained serious damage and it was closed for good in 1924. In 2003 a brand new replica line (including locomotive and carriages) was opened as a tourist attraction and museum, about 100 metres from the site of the original site in Listowel; operating on 1,000 metres of track, it is well worth the visit if you are in the area.

Not very far away from the replica, a local man had spent about fifty years tracking down any parts of the original monorail that he could and has been able to collect about 50 metres of track and an original carriage. First class carriage No. 5 is pictured on 15 April 2017. Unfortunately, due to ill health the gentleman has been unable in recent years to maintain the vehicle and it is becoming rather dilapidated (on the far side it has fallen apart). The good news is that the people at Listowel have been in touch with the man and his family, and it looks like the carriage and track might be donated to them to display in the museum, preserving a vital part of Ireland's transport history for many years to come.

In 1887 a narrow gauge (3-foot) railway opened in County Cork in southern Ireland to take advantage of tourist traffic to and from Blarney Castle (home of the legendary Blarney Stone). The railway operated westwards from Cork at Western Road Station for 6.5 miles to Coachford Junction, then a further 2 miles to the castle. In 1888 a further 9-mile extension was opened westward from Coachford Junction to a terminus station at Coachford. Later, in 1893, a further 8.5-mile extension was opened from the junction to Donaghmore. The railway became part of the Great Southern Railway in 1925 and was closed at the end of December in 1934.

Carriages from this railway were sold upon its closure and many were used as holiday homes in the coastal areas around Cork. This example is one of the few that still survive, as most were scrapped and replaced with new houses or static caravans. Numbered 1, it was built by the Oldbury Carriage & Wagon Company in 1887. It was photographed on 28 April 2018, when it was still being used as a holiday home at Cox's Field, which is on the old road (R634) between Cork and Youghal.

The Great Southern Railways operated in the Republic of Ireland between 1925 and 1945, when it became incorporated into the Córas Iompair Éireann. This carriage was built by the railway at their Inchicore works, which is situated on the western outskirts of Dublin, as a first-class open in 1935 and was numbered 1144. In 1973 the CIÉ converted it for use as a mobile classroom and numbered it 586A in their departmental number series. The Cavan & Leitrim Railway, based at Dromod in County Leitrim, purchased the vehicle in 1997 and grounded the body for use as a tea room. It was pictured being used as such on 26 April 2018.

During January 1853, the business community of Waterford financed the building of an independent railway connecting the city to the seaside resort of Tramore, some 7.25 miles away, at a cost of £77,000. Work began in February of that year and by the beginning of September the line opened to the public, barely seven months after construction began. The railway was amalgamated into the Great Southern Railway in 1925 and subsequently part of the Córas Iompair Éireann (CIÉ). It was the CIÉ who finally decided to close the line, doing so at the end of December 1960.

Rolling stock from this railway is extremely rare. However, on 28 April 2018 these two examples were found near Ballyvoyle, adjacent to the Deise Greenway (which is a 46-km trail that runs along a former railway line trackbed between Waterford and Dungarvan, featuring eleven bridges, three viaducts and a 400-metre tunnel).

These two coaches had been used as a holiday home overlooking the sea until the mid-1990s. Since then, they have sadly become the target for vandals and arsonists. The one nearest the camera is No. 8 and is in slightly better condition than the one behind it, which is No. 13. They were both built in the mid-1850s and were used on the railway until its closure. As with the Cork & Muskerry coaches the majority of vehicles from this railway ended up as holiday homes along the coast between Waterford and Tramore, but sadly these two appear to be the only remaining survivors.

A failed preservation movement in Ireland, Westrail Ltd were based in Tuam, County Galway. They were formed in 1985 and ran preserved trains between Athenry, Tuam and Claremorris; however, the company was dissolved in 2004. The majority of the stock they owned was dispersed, although some items were scrapped on site.

This vehicle was built by the CIÉ in 1954 as a composite and numbered 2153; following its conversion to a standard brake vehicle in 1976 it was re-numbered to 1934. It was withdrawn from service in 1982 and was acquired by Westrail in 1986. Following the demise of that operating company it was moved to the Cavan & Leitrim Railway at Dromod in 2005, where its body was grounded and used as a book shop and store shed. It was seen at that location, placed end to end with GSR carriage No. 1144, on 26 April 2018.

CHAPTER 5

British Railways Passenger Carriages

In January 1948 the railways were nationalised and British Railways (BR) was formed. Just like the companies at Grouping in 1923, BR also inherited large numbers of post-Grouping passenger vehicles and promptly began to build carriages to a uniform design, which eventually led to the older vehicles becoming redundant and either being scrapped or sold to preservation groups/societies. There are still a few bodies from 1948 onwards that remain today, seeing various uses.

Built by the Birmingham Railway Carriage & Wagon Company for British Railways in 1956, this was Mk I tourist second open carriage No. 4288. It was withdrawn from service by BR in 1973 and sold to the Dart Valley Railway in Buckfastleigh, Devon. In 1984 the body (along with three others) was sold to Watermouth Castle Estates and in 1985 they were moved to the former LSWR Mortehoe & Woolacombe station, which had been sitting empty and derelict for fifteen years since its closure in 1970.

The bodies were placed end to end, where they would become part of the 'Once Upon A Time' children's adventure and theme park. Two of them were used to house a museum of children's stories and a display area, while the other two were used to house a play pen and crèche (including a soft-play ball pit, which was three-quarters the length of one of the vehicles). This theme park also included an LMSR fish van body as a go-kart store shed and a few BR 'vanwide' bodies as various store sheds (one even housed a pets' corner – with rabbits, guinea pigs and pygmy goats). At the time of my visit on 11 March 2000, the park was closed for the winter season; however, within five years the theme park had closed permanently, and all the railway vehicles were scrapped on site by a contractor by 2006.

No. 4427 was a British Railways Mk I tourist second open. Built by the BRC&W in 1956, it was withdrawn after twenty-nine years of service in 1985. Its body was sold to the owners of a 228-year-old former cattle drovers' inn, The Leadburn Inn at West Linton in Peebles, Midlothian, where it was used as a restaurant. The picture, which was taken on 3 August 2004, still shows it carrying its number (complete with its SC prefix, which denoted that it operated on the Scottish Region).

Sadly, in November 2005 disaster was to strike the inn, when a car veered off the road at about 9 a.m., ploughing through a hedge and a conservatory before hitting a wall. This in itself would not have been too devastating, but the chain of events that followed was. After hitting the wall the car burst into flames, which then quickly spread to the pub's wooden beams. Before long the pub was engulfed in fire, which took five crews nearly six hours to get under control. Unfortunately, the thirty-six-year-old driver of the car lost his life. The pub had to be totally demolished, while the carriage was beyond repair and was subsequently scrapped. Fortunately, there were no guests staying at the inn at the time, or else the death toll would have been much worse. The inn was rebuilt in 2010 and continues to be an enjoyable place for people to meet, eat, drink and stay.

Mk II tourist second open No. 5324 was built by BR at Derby carriage works in 1968. After twenty years of service it was withdrawn and the body was preserved by the Quainton Road Society Limited and taken to their base in Buckinghamshire, where it served as a society office for eleven years. It was then turned into a sales coach for the restoration of GWR steam locomotive No. 6989 *Wightwick Hall*, and it was pictured in this guise on 15 August 2010.

The majority of carriages that ended up in a scrapyard left as nothing more than pieces of metal that would go for recycling. However, this was not the case for this 1962 BR-built vehicle from Derby. No. 25911 (later re-numbered to 18911 in the late 1970s/early 1980s), a Mk I corridor second-class vehicle, was withdrawn from service in 1989. It was sold to Vic Berry Ltd (who specialised in asbestos removal) and was transported by rail to Braunstone Gate goods yard, just outside of Leicester, on the former Great Central Railway. In 1990 the body – complete with its underframe, but without the bogies – was purchased from Berry's yard by members of the Bekonscot Model Village Society, with it then being taken to their site at Beaconsfield in Buckinghamshire. I took this picture of it there on 12 August 2017, where it was being used as a shop and ticket office for the model village and miniature railway.

In 1985 a new hotel complex was built adjacent to the East Coast Main Line at Shipton-by-Beningbrough, about 5 miles north of York. The hotel, known as The Sidings, was the brainchild of a former railwayman who had a passion and enthusiasm for all things related to railways, and who wanted people to partake in the 'ultimate railway experience'. The hotel is built around the bodies of five former British Railways Mk I carriages that were built in the 1950s, with the bodies being converted into a dining room, a sitting room/lounge (complete with a fully stocked bar) and bedrooms. One of these vehicles is this corridor third, No. 24676, which was built by the Cravens Railway Carriage & Wagon Company Ltd in Darnall, Sheffield, in 1953. It is used as part of the bedroom section (nearest the camera) and the sitting room/lounge and was pictured on 6 April 2012.

CHAPTER 6

Pre-Grouping Non-Passenger-Carrying Coaching Stock Vehicles

A brief explanation is required here. Passenger carriages, which I have covered in the first five chapters, are self-explanatory, in that they are vehicles that carry passengers. However, non-passenger-carrying coaching stock (NPCCS) is a little more complex.

There are some vehicles in this category that are used as the braking vehicle within a train's consist. They are divided into two categories, which are 'passenger brakes' and 'full brakes'. The passenger brake vehicles contain the braking compartment used by the train's guard, and they can also carry passengers in them as well, but they still come under the NPCCS umbrella. The full brake vehicles do not carry any passengers at all; they only have the braking compartment and room for certain goods, such as heavy items of luggage or bicycles, etc.

There are other anomalies in this category: milk tanks are included but not water tanks; some types of fruit vans are, but not banana vans; and vehicles that look like freight wagons but are not also fall under the banner. It can be difficult to ascertain which vehicles belong in the NPCCS category or under the freight stock categorisation.

Companies Amalgamated into the Great Western Railway (GWR)

The grounded bodies of non-passenger-carrying vehicles from any of the constituent companies that became part of the GWR are extremely rare. In fact, at the time of writing I have only managed to find one of these vehicles. Having said that, I have found examples of GWR vehicles that were built before the pre-Grouping era, and these are included here.

This artist's studio, pictured at a farm in Cornwall on 14 June 2014, began its working life in 1895 at the Gloucester Carriage & Wagon Company as a six-wheeled, six-compartment, third-class vehicle for the Barry Railway and was numbered 38. In 1909 it was converted to a three-compartment luggage brake third, before being acquired by the GWR in 1923. It was withdrawn in December 1927 and by May the following year the body was transported to its current resting place, where it was used as holiday accommodation until the late 1990s, when it became a storage shed and was looking in poor condition. It was smartened up considerably and became the artist's studio in 2012.

In 1880 the original GWR built this four-wheeled passenger luggage van (No. 59) at its Swindon works. It was withdrawn from service in 1934 and was grounded on the platform at Morebath Junction station in Devon, where it was used by passengers as a shelter from the elements. During the 1950s the body was purchased by a Mr Chown, who transported it using a tractor and trailer the 4 miles to his house at Petton Cross. It was used for over thirty years as a hay store for his cattle, but in the mid-1980s Mr Chown gave up the cattle and it then saw use as a log store. At the time of my visit, on 23 May 1996, it was still being used as such. Sadly, the body was scrapped during 2002, when new owners acquired the house.

This vehicle is a covered carriage truck, so named due to the double set of doors that are found at each end, which could enable a small car to be driven into one end and out of the other. The car would be secured while being transported by ropes or chains, which were attached to eyelets located within the sides of the vehicle. This particular example was built by the Great Western Railway at Swindon in 1870. Numbered 109, it was withdrawn from service two years after Grouping, in 1925. Its body was then sold and transported to Mill Lane in Box, where it was used as a garage, and it was still being used as such when seen on 12 May 1997.

Companies Amalgamated into the London, Midland & Scottish Railway (LMS)

The bodies of the constituent companies that fall within this category are fairly slim, but examples do exist. In some instances, extremely rare examples have survived (albeit only just with some of them).

This covered carriage truck (CCT) was built by the LNWR at Wolverton in 1922 and was numbered 12220. It was re-numbered twice while under the ownership of the LMS (first to No. 4207 in 1928 and then again to No. 36992 in 1933). In 1957 it was transferred into the Midland Region departmental fleet series as No. DM395273. It was used by Messrs Pooley & Sons as one of their weighing test vehicles before being preserved by the Historic Rolling Stock Group in 1973. It was then sold to the 2857 Society, who were based on the Severn Valley Railway, where it remained as a mobile workshop until 1982, when it moved to Peak Rail at Buxton, before being sold to the Somerset & Dorset Trust Museum at Washford station on the West Somerset Railway. Its underframe was donated for the temporary storage of one of the S&D coach bodies that was undergoing restoration; however, its length was deemed unsuitable and it was re-sold to another society. Meanwhile, the body was grounded and used as a visitor centre, which is how it was pictured on 31 May 2008. Note the unusual shape of the top of the double doors on the end – typical of LNWR vehicles of this type.

Pictured at Cucklington in Somerset on 14 March 2012 is this Lancashire & Yorkshire Railway six-wheeled, three-compartment 'Birdgage' luggage brake third, which was numbered 571. It was built at Newton Heath in Manchester in 1882, and by 1916 it had been purchased along with seven others by the Barry Railway and re-numbered 227. Following the railway's amalgamation with the GWR in 1923, it was re-numbered 242 and it was withdrawn from service in 1927. Following withdrawal, this vehicle was one of six that became used as dwellings at Milton Damerel, near Barnstaple in North Devon, with this one being the only current survivor of the six. It has since been used as a holiday home to let. Interesting, all three numbers it carried were found on the inside during its restoration process. The term 'Birdgage' relates to vehicles such as this where the guard has lookouts on the sides of the vehicles but also a raised roof with windows on it (sometimes this can be in the middle of the vehicle or on the end as can be seen in this picture).

Companies Amalgamated into the London & North Eastern Railway (LNER)

As with the two previous companies, the bodies from vehicles of this era are a little bit thin on the ground, but there are some excellent examples of complete vehicles at preservation sites and museums.

Four-wheeled passenger train-cattle truck No.33 was built at Stratford works in East London for the Great Eastern Railway in 1892. It was defined as an NPCCS, because it was specifically built to be used among passenger trains and it was therefore not regarded as freight stock. In around 1910 it was partially converted to a fruit and fish van, which was done by filling in the upper section of the body with narrow slats (it would have previously just been an open space all along the sides at the top). It was re-numbered three more times before being withdrawn in 1928, being grounded as a mess hut at Melton Yard in Suffolk. It was preserved and taken to the Mangapps Farm Railway Museum in Burnham-on-Crouch, Essex, in 1991. Three years later it was mounted onto the underframe of an ex-GER van body and was taken for display at Old Heath station, where it was pictured on 15 June 2013.

The Great North of Scotland Railway was formed in 1845 and ran the 39 miles between Kittybrewster and the small town of Huntly (where the castle gave refuge to Robert the Bruce, among others). At Grouping it was one of the two smallest of the five major companies in Scotland that became part of the LNER. Being one of the smallest companies hasn't prevented a rather surprising amount of its vehicles being found as grounded bodies, however. There were approximately sixty that were known and recorded, although there may well be others as yet undiscovered. Of those sixty, about a dozen or so have since been scrapped.

No. 6 was built in 1890 at the company's Kittybrewster works, and was a six-wheeled full brake vehicle (note the guard's lookouts on the body side). Little else is known about this vehicle, only that its body was preserved in 1985 and taken to Lochty, and later Methil Yard, before finally ending up in a yard adjacent to the current Kingdom of Fife Railway Preservation Society at Leven, which was where I photographed it on 4 August 2004. By April 2017, however, the body is believed to have been damaged by fire and is beyond salvaging, but confirmation of this is required by the author at time of writing.

Companies Amalgamated into the Southern Railway (SR)

Very few of these vehicles can be found as grounded bodies, but the ones that have been found are quite interesting, and sometimes rare.

Looking at a house like this, you would think it rather odd to have an unusually shaped piece of concrete on the side which doesn't seem to serve any purpose. This is another giveaway clue that there is a railway carriage beneath the concrete, as the unusual shape was actually the guard's lookout and there would have been a window on each side to enable the guard to see clearly along the length of the train. This example started off life in the late 1880s, probably at Brighton for the LB&SCR as a three-compartment, third-class brake van, which would have contained a large wheel that the guard would use to stop the train. It was pictured at Pagham on 19 May 2018.

This former six-wheeled, 30-foot full brake (with central guard's caboose), that was built in 1884 and numbered 389, was an L&SWR vehicle. Re-numbered 4595 in about 1903/04, it was still carrying both numbers internally when I visited and took this picture on 26 November 2006. The vehicle was withdrawn from service in June 1917 and was sold to a gentleman in Winchester, who used it as a shed on an allotment. In 1928 the body was purchased and moved to Dewey's Lane, Ludgershall, between Devizes and Andover in Wiltshire, and was used as a dwelling (as seen). However, by 2009 the vehicle was scrapped following planning permission having been granted for a new house to be built on the site. It is such a pity that the body was not donated to a preservation society or a museum, due to it being the last surviving (at the time) L&SWR full brake.

On 6 April 1998, I was fortunate to come across this vehicle in Highbridge, Somerset. It is a Somerset & Dorset Joint Railway parcels van that was built in approximately 1860 at the S&DJR works in Highbridge and was designated No. 9; it was used to transport parcels and perishable goods between the stations on the Wells branch. It was withdrawn from service in 1926 and was pulled from Highbridge station to its location here, adjacent to the main line. Originally used as a hay store, it later became used as a lambing shed and then as a general store. In 2000 it was rumoured to have been donated to the S&D Trust at Washford for eventual restoration, but it is uncertain whether this ever materialised, or if the vehicle even survived the move, as there seems to be no further mention of it anywhere.

This parcels & miscellaneous van (PMV) was built at Ashford works in Kent for the SE&CR in 1922 and was given the number 155. Following Grouping it was re-numbered 1996 by the SR. It continued in revenue-earning service until 1962, when it was taken into the departmental fleet for the Southern Region and became a control train generator van, being re-numbered DS70165. It was later seen at the engineers' sidings in Ashford and later still the body was grounded at the nearby crane workshops. In 1994 it was purchased and transferred to the Mangapps Farm Railway Museum in Essex, where it was used as a steam loco department stores van, and where it was photographed on 15 June 2013.

CHAPTER 7

Post-Grouping Non-Passenger-Carrying Coaching Stock Vehicles

Great Western Railway (GWR)

Examples of vehicles found within this category built by the GWR include horse boxes and fish, fruit, and luggage vans. Some of the vehicles found have since been scrapped or are in a very poor condition.

This book shop and antiquary, located at the Great Western Society Railway Centre in Didcot, was built at Swindon in approximately 1934 and was originally a six-wheeled tool van that was numbered in the departmental fleet series as DW109. It was withdrawn from service during the 1960s and was preserved at Didcot. In 1973 the body was grounded in the spot where I photographed it on 17 April 2010 and its underframe was used to mount the body of one of the society's rescued GWR passenger coaches for resoration.

Railway companies tended to give generic names to their rolling stock based on certain types, and the GWR was no exception in this. They gave the name 'Python' to their covered carriage trucks (sometimes a suffix letter would be added to a certain class; Python-B for example). During the early years of the twentieth century and right up until the late 1960s/early 1970s, circuses were at the height of their popularity in this country, and as result of this special trains were created that would carry the entire entourage from town to town (including the big top, side stalls and the animals, which were one of the biggest attractions). After arriving at the station, more often than not the circus would be paraded through the streets of the town to the site where they would set up for the duration of the time they were to be performing there.

Built at Swindon in 1914, this Python, No. 580, was a one-off build that was especially strengthened to carry circus elephants. This involved putting concrete on the floor, while special tethering rings were fitted to the floor and heavy chains were included. Additionally, the glass from the windows was removed and replaced with strong steel bars, giving the animals an adequate air supply during transportation. It was pictured on 14 April 2012 in Ponthirwaun, central Wales, where it was out of use, but it had previously been used to store some of the owner's vintage tractor collection.

This vehicle was another one built by the GWR (and, like so many others, was pre-Grouping). It was built in 1889 as a Travelling Post Office and was numbered 599. Built on broad gauge bogies, it had a narrow (standard) gauge body. Despite the 'Gauge War' having being resolved some thirty-five years earlier, there were some smaller lines that still had broad gauge tracks on them – which showed the slow progress and reluctance on the part of Brunel to change the gauge on his railway, despite it being made compulsory to do so.

It was finally converted to standard gauge in 1891, which just meant putting different bogies on it as the body was already in line with the standard gauge. It was then re-numbered 2086. In 1896 it was converted from a TPO to an ordinary mail coach and was re-numbered again to 841. By 1909 it had been fitted with a lavatory and it was to run in service until 1934. Upon its withdrawal it was transported by road to a remote hillside farmhouse in the mountains just west of Llangurig in Powys, Wales, which was where I photographed it on 16 June 1999.

Vehicles of this type are extremely rare to find. This example was built in 1952 and was categorised as a 'Beetle C' – though this has nothing whatsoever to do with transporting Volkswagen Beetles! Numbered 751, these vehicles were specifically used to carry prize-winning cattle and were similar to horse boxes, except that the drover's compartment was situated in the middle, between the two cattle compartments (as indicated by the two central doors in the picture). In 1971, when it was withdrawn from service, the body was purchased by Michael Toop, who was a dealer from Frome in Somerset that specialised in transporting bodies of railway vehicles to his customers. This body (along with a SR cattle van) was transported to Southfield House, near Whatley. The picture, which was taken on 23 October 1999, shows the intact side; the other side has had the cattle compartment doors and drop-down ramps removed and replaced with two-thirds-high plywood doors for its use as a stable.

One type of vehicle that is seldom seen as grounded bodies is the GWR 'Siphon' covered milk van. These vehicles were built specially for the conveyance of milk. Previously, milk churns had been collected in open wagons and conveyed within freight trains. However, freight trains are given a low priority and are often put into sidings to allow passenger trains to pass. Sometimes during peak periods and in the high summer months, those freight trains could be sat in a siding for several hours, and this would result in the milk going off. In introducing these specially built vans that could be carried within passenger trains, the milk was able to arrive at its destination much more quickly than before.

The first of these vehicles came into use in 1870. The sides of the vehicle consisted of slats of wood with large gaps between them, thus allowing air to circulate around the churns. These vehicles were also used for the conveyance of fish packed with ice. By 1907, the year that this vehicle was built (and designated 'Siphon C'), using these vans for carrying fish ceased and purpose-built fish vans were constructed. This vehicle was numbered 1540 and it was withdrawn in 1947, where it was conveyed the 3 miles from the nearby Newtown station in Powys, using two Fordson Standard 'N' tractors and a hay trailer, to its location at Aberbechan Dike, where it was photographed on 19 April 2003, mounted onto stone wall type slabs and used as a general store shed.

Another example of the 'Siphon' vehicle, the 'Siphon G' was the first type of this vehicle to have corridor connections, therefore enabling the churns to be positioned while the train was moving, in readiness so that when the next station was reached, the relevant churns could be offloaded quickly and not inconvenience the passengers with lengthy delays. This example, No. 1267, was built in 1927 at Swindon. Later, in September 1958, it became a service vehicle and was numbered 064721 in the Western Region Internal User number series. Its final withdrawal came in 1961 and it was sold to Woodham's scrapyard in Barry the following year.

While on the lookout for a pen to house his sheep in, especially during lambing season, a farmer was told by a friend that he could get a goods van body or something similar from Woodham's yard, so he made the trip down to Barry to see what he could buy. Upon his arrival, he noticed that this vehicle had already begun to be cut up, so he told Dai that he would take the remaining half, which he did. On the following day it was transported the 86 miles to his remote hillside location just north of Llanybydder in Carmarthenshire, where it was still being used to house sheep when I photographed it on 8 April 1999.

Built in Swindon in 1948, this six-wheeled insulated fish van was one of a batch of fifty specially built by the GWR. This vehicle, No. 3345, was one of several of the batch that were transferred to Scotland following the fall in fish traffic on the GWR and the increase in fish traffic from places such as Aberdeen and Fraserburgh during the 1950s and '60s. It was withdrawn from service in 1969 and its body was acquired and taken to a farm in Ironhill, near Rosehearty, Aberdeenshire, to be used as a general storage shed; in fact, it was still being used as such on 27 March 2016, when I visited. Note the four iceboxes still in situ on the roof of the vehicle. These were used for refrigeration when it was used to transport fish.

London, Midland & Scottish Railway (LMS)

The bodies of LMS vehicles mostly seem to come from either fish vans or fruit and milk vans, although there are also horse boxes and passenger brakes. The number of vehicles in this category is relatively small, but several complete vehicles are to be found at preservation sites across the country.

The LMS only built two types of non-passenger-carrying livestock vehicles: horse boxes and prize cattle vans. The last batch of 145 horse boxes built by the company was something of an oddity, in that the first twenty-five were built at York in 1954 and the remaining 120 were built at Earlstown in 1955. These vehicles were built to an LNER design and were numbered in the LNER number series. This particular example was one of the Earlstown-built vehicles and was numbered 2470. It was withdrawn in 1975, at which point it was taken to a farm in Smalley, Derbyshire, where it became a stable for Shetland ponies (hence the low wooden fence around the door nearest the camera). At the time of my visit there during the Whitsun Bank Holiday weekend on 26 May 2003, it had been out of use for about five years, and it was finally scrapped on site seven years later, in 2010. Note that the 'torpedo' roof ventilators are still in situ.

Gangwayed full brake vehicles built by the LMS are quite popular as grounded bodies. This example was built in 1941 at Wolverton works in Buckinghamshire and was numbered 31255. It was withdrawn from service in 1982 and its body was acquired from the Marple & Gillott scrapyard in Sheffield during 1983 by the Great Central Railway. It was grounded at the rear of Loughborough engine shed and was used as a shop by the Rothley Carriage & Wagon department, as can be seen by the books and videos on shelves inside the door from this 21 November 2009 photograph. It was scrapped on site in 2013.

This vehicle, another gangwayed full brake carriage, was numbered 31926 when it was built at Wolverton works in 1944. It remained in service until 1986 and was bought for preservation by the Northampton & Lamport Railway Society, being taken to their site at Pitsford. In 1996 the railway was approached by the owners of the former Castle Ashby station in Northamptonshire, who enquired whether they had any vehicles going spare as they were after another vehicle to go with the two that they already had in use as part of a restaurant. The railway sold them this body, which was then used as a residence, so that that the owners could live on site. It was photographed by myself on 13 October 2012.

As described earlier, the GWR had purpose-built vans that were designed to carry milk. The LMS also had vehicles built that were for carrying milk, although they weren't restricted to just carrying milk, but also conveyed fruit as well. This is one of those vehicles; it was built in 1926 and numbered 38005 (it was re-numbered to 38305 in 1933). It was withdrawn from service in 1961 and its body ended up as an office on an allotments in Pleasley Hill, Nottinghamshire which was where it was pictured on 23 March 2004. Note how the top half of the body is slatted to allow air to circulate, thus helping to keep the contents (mostly the fruit) fresh. These vehicles were built with two metal vents on each end which were slatted beneath them; however, all the bodies of these vehicles that I have found have been missing the right hand end vent and this vehicle is no exception to that. Upon re-visiting the site again in June 2016, it was discovered that the body was no longer in situ and was believed to have been broken up between eight and ten years previously.

London & North Eastern Railway (LNER)

Despite being the second largest company of the Big Four, non-passenger-carrying vehicles are not well represented in terms of the numbers that have survived. In fact, there are fewer vehicles of this category left than any of the other three companies.

This six-wheeled covered carriage truck, No. 1349, was built at Darlington in 1950. As you can see, the LNER versions of these vehicles had three sliding doors on the sides and a set of double doors on each end. This vehicle was withdrawn in 1968 and was sent for scrap at Birds Ltd of Long Marston. The body (complete with underframe) was moved a few hundred yards further along the road, to Marston Grange, where it was used as a general storage shed, as when seen on my visit there on 9 December 1995. As well as the underframe, the vehicle had its torpedo roof ventilators intact, and was in remarkably good condition when I saw it. However, a photograph of it taken in 2011 shows planks missing from the door nearest the camera, with the roof felt all gone and holes in its body, so it was not surprising to hear that it was scrapped on site in 2015.

This four-wheeled plywood fish van was built at the Faverdale Wagon Works in Darlington in 1948. This vehicle, No. 75065, and the vehicle seen beside it to the right (built in 1949) were both built by British Railways and were among the last vehicles to be built to an LNER design, with BR having their own designs built from 1950 onwards. Both of these vehicles were withdrawn from service in 1983, when BR took the decision that all vehicles built prior to Nationalisation and those built to Grouping companies' designs should be removed from the rail network (with the exception of a small amount used as departmental stock). The bodies were sold and taken to a remote farmyard near Easter Aulton in Aberdeenshire for use as store sheds. At the time of my visit, on 26 March 2016, they were both in a poor state and out of use, as can be seen in the picture.

Designed by Sir Nigel Gresley, who was the Chief Mechanical Engineer of the LNER, this 1938 gangwayed full brake vehicle was built at York. These vehicles are also referred to as 'Pigeon Vans', due to them being used for the transportation of racing pigeons in baskets, which were held on shelves fitted within the carriage.

This example began its working life as No. 4237. It was re-numbered 70460 in 1946, and in the early 1970s it was taken into the departmental stock fleet, being numbered DB975242 accordingly. Withdrawn in 1980, it was purchased by the Steamtown Railway Museum at the former Carnforth Motive Power Depot site, where the body was grounded and used as a polisher's store and workshop. By the end of the 1997 season it was decided that Steamtown would close as a tourist attraction, having operated for thirty years. However, in June 1998 a new company operating as the West Coast Railway Company took over the former MPD site as a repair and operating facility which was not open to the general public. In 2008 an enthusiasts' open weekend took place at the site and I took this picture there on Saturday 26 July, showing the body still in situ but now out of use. The body was sold to the newly formed Poulton & Wyre Railway Society and moved to their site at Thornton Cleveleys, near Blackpool, in 2014, being placed onto a set of bogies.

Southern Railway (SR)

The number of bodies from this company is far greater than any of the other three, with the majority of these being either covered carriage trucks (CCT) or parcels & miscellaneous vans (PMV). Many of these vehicles can be found at preservation sites across the country, several of which have had the body removed (and either been scrapped or used as stores), while the underframes have been used to carry bodies that have been restored or are awaiting restoration (*see Chapter 19*).

While bodies of passenger-carrying vehicles from the Southern Railway do not appear to remain in existence, the same cannot be said of the NPCCS vehicles, with an abundance of covered carriage trucks (CCTs) and parcels and miscellaneous vans (PMVs) surviving. Weston-super-Mare AFC, who play in the National League South, were formed in 1948, and they play at the Woodsping Stadium on Winterstoke Road in Weston, North Somerset. Prior to moving to this new ground in 2004, they played a short distance away, at a ground at Woodspring Park that was built almost entirely by the club's supporters. Part of that ground included this 1947-built Southern Railway PMV, numbered 1538. It was withdrawn in 1982 and was purchased by the supporters of the club the following year, to be used as the club shop, as pictured here on 12 September 1998. It was scrapped on site by 2006, when the former ground was redeveloped as a housing estate.

Earlier in this chapter I mentioned that the majority of vehicles built to Grouping companies' designs ended in 1950, when BR built their own designed vehicles. This was not always the case, however, and some vehicles were still being produced from Grouping company designs up until the mid-1950s. This CCT was one such vehicle. It was built at Lancing works, Sussex, in 1955 by BR to a SR design and was even numbered into the SR number series as 2524.

Like many vehicles it was withdrawn in 1984, and in 1987 it was purchased (along with two other CCT vehicles) by the narrow gauge Brecon Mountain Railway. All three bodies were taken to the operating base of the railway at Pontsticill in Powys, where they were laid end to end in a line. The body, seen here on 23 May 1999, and the one adjacent to it each had one end removed and formed part of the café and shop, while the third body was converted into the toilet facilities. The four end vents are still clearly visible on the set of double doors.

CHAPTER 8

Irish Railways Non-Passenger-Carrying Coaching Stock Vehicles

The railway companies in Ireland never had large numbers of vehicles of this category, and so only minimal amounts have survive, either as bodies or complete vehicles. As a result, those that have survived are regarded as extremely rare vehicles indeed, and should be treated as such.

Following an Act of Parliament in 1906, which authorised the purchase of three companies (the Donegal Railway Company, the Great Northern Railway of Ireland and the Midland Railway Northern Counties Committee), the County Donegal Railways Joint Committee was formed. The company initially ran 106 miles of narrow gauge track, but by 1909 the Strabane & Letterkenny Railway was opened, which extended their running lines to 121 miles. Following dieselisation, between 1930 and 1951 eleven railcars (eight of them articulated) were built by Walker Brothers of Wigan, and these were the only vehicles operating on the system until 1960, when the railway was closed.

They only ran a small fleet, which, prior to the First World War, consisted of twenty-one locomotives, fifty-six carriages and a surprising 304 freight vehicles. As a result, surviving vehicles from this railway are fairly rare. Built in 1934, this vehicle, No. 12, despite looking like a freight goods van, was actually a passenger luggage van trailer. These trailers were built for carrying luggage and were lighter than the usual freight vehicles to enable them to be towed behind the diesel railcars. This example was pictured on 7 April 2015 at the Donegal Railway Restoration Ltd Museum in Donegal, looking rather faded and in need of a re-paint.

In 1875 the Londonderry & Enniskillen and the Enniskillen & Bundoran railways merged to form the Sligo, Leitrim & Northern Counties Railway, operating in the north-west of Ireland in Cavan, Fermanagh, Leitrim and Sligo. It was not absorbed into the Great Southern Railway of Ireland because it crossed the border into the North. Sadly, the railway never really prospered due to the countryside it passed through being so sparsely populated, and it closed in 1957.

Surviving vehicles from this railway are few and far between; a couple of diesel railcars and steam locomotives are preserved, but as for bodies this example is the only one I have come across at the time of writing. It may not look like it, but this vehicle began life as prize cattle wagon No. 240. Built in 1892, it would have been used on passenger trains. A sizeable number of these vehicles were built, as the number of cattle being transported often outnumbered the passengers. No. 240 was acquired in the 1990s from a farm by the Ulster Folk & Transport Museum at Cultra, near Belfast. It was pictured in an area not open to the general public on a specially permitted visit on 4 April 2015, to the rear of the restoration workshops. There it waits to be mounted onto the underframe of a nearby open goods wagon, and then it can be fully restored and put on display in the museum.

CHAPTER 9

British Railways Non-Passenger-Carrying Coaching Stock Vehicles

Built by BR after Nationalisation in 1948, the most frequently found body types in this category are fish vans and fruit vans. There are also a reasonable number of general utility vehicles (GUVs), covered carriage trucks (CCTs) and passenger brake vehicles.

Built by BR at Earlestown in Merseyside in 1954, this was a four-wheeled insulated 'blue spot' fish van, No. 87554. To ensure the fish reached their destination in as fresh a condition as possible, a large blue circle was painted on both sides of the body, hence the name 'blue spot', and this guaranteed the vehicles were put into express passenger train consists. The bodies were plywood skinned with smooth aluminium sheets (which made cleaning the inside easier), while the roofs comprised two skins of aluminium that were filled with a rubber insulation material known as Ozanote. The doors were draught-proofed and due to the fish being packed with water ice there were two drains in the floor to prevent the vehicle from flooding. The interiors of the vehicles were kept cool with numerous boxes of dry ice. Like all fish vans, they were painted white to reflect the heat away from the vehicle.

In 1968, when fish traffic declined, a good many vehicles were transferred for use as express parcels vans. Some were taken into internal service and were used as mobile or static stores if the body was grounded at a works or depot. This example was withdrawn in 1970 and became a grounded stores van at Woking yard. It was purchased in 2004 and transported to Okehampton station in Devon to be used as a cycle hire store (note the ramp that has been built to allow the cycles to be easily wheeled in and out). It was photographed on 30 June 2007.

This vehicle was built at Swindon in 1958 as a four-wheeled fruit van (classified as a 'Fruit-D') and numbered 92111. It was withdrawn in 1982 and, along with five other bodies, it was purchased and taken to Manor Farm in Ilmington, Warwickshire. There they were used as general store sheds, as can be seen in this picture, which was taken on 22 February 2003. By June 2005, five out of the six bodies (including this one) had become so badly dilapidated that they were scrapped on site by the owner.

This four-wheeled covered carriage truck was built at Earlestown in 1960 and was numbered 94344. Following its withdrawal from service in the late 1970s, it was grounded at Crewe Diesel Depot as a store and was numbered into the Midland Region Internal User series as 024457. In 1988 it was purchased by a farmer in Talerddig, Powys, and was transported to his farm, where it was turned into a boiler shed, with a fully functioning workshop in one half and a lambing pen in the other. In this photograph, taken on 7 September 2008, the lambing pen can be seen to have been fitted with a wood burner (as heat is a necessity where new-born lambs are concerned). The external chimney for this can be seen on the side of the vehicle.

CHAPTER 10

London Underground Tube Cars

Odd though it may seem, several former London Underground Tube car bodies have been purchased after becoming surplus to requirements. Those numbers have seen an increase in recent years, mostly due to two main factors, which are:

1. As the older cars are being replaced with brand-new modern 'open-plan' trains, the vehicles become either stockpiled at various depots throughout the underground system or at scrapyards.
2. The bodies of these vehicles are lighter and less cumbersome than main line vehicles and are therefore easier to transport.

Hamleys Toy Shop in Regent Street, London, is renowned as being one of the biggest and best toy shops in Europe. In the lower ground floor of the store could be found the cab of a 1972-built Northern Line driving motor car, No. 3214, which was part of the attraction of 'all things London'. While visiting the store with his grandchildren on 10 June 2014, a very good friend of mine, Stuart Davidson, took this photograph of the cab, which he gave to me, knowing that I had an interest in all things railway related. Sadly he passed away in 2016. When I was looking through my photograph collection for pictures to put in this book, I came across this one taken by Stuart, and asked his widow if I could use it in this book. She readily agreed, with her blessing.

In December 2017 I paid a visit to the toy store, finding that the whole lower ground floor was now dedicated to the *Star Wars* movie franchise, and that the front of the car had been completely removed, with what remained made to represent a stormtrooper's pod, complete with life-sized stormtrooper models in front of it to allow fans to have their photograph taken with them. The remainder of the vehicle is used to store toys and other memorabilia of the franchise, and it is virtually impossible to tell that it was ever an Underground car.

Built by Metro-Cammell in 1988, this was stock driving motor No. 3634. It worked on the Jubilee line until it was withdrawn in 2002, when it was intended to go to the London Transport Museum at Covent Garden. However, this never materialised and the body was reduced by about a third in length and was taken to the Great Ormond Street Children's Hospital, where it was pictured on 20 April 2013. The body is used as the hospital's Radio Lollipop broadcasting station and as an activity centre for the patients.

Mounted on part of a former North London Railway viaduct high above the East London streets in Holywell Lane, Shoreditch, is the Village Underground. This complex is part creative community and part arts venue, and also contains the bodies of four ex-Jubilee line Underground cars that are used as offices and art studios. The Village Underground also took over an old warehouse adjacent to the viaduct, which was formerly used as a coal store by the railway and which is now used as a concert venue.

The four cars were all built by Metro-Cammell in 1988. Consisting of two driving motors and two trailers, they were numbered 3662, 3733, 4633 and 4662. They were transported by road to the site in 2006, with them then being craned into position on top of the former viaduct section; the road in the area was closed to traffic for the whole day while this took place. On 19 May 2012 I visited the site, but sadly the complex was not open as it was a weekend, so I was unable to get close to the cars. I did take this picture from the nearby London Overground station, however, which shows all four vehicles in situ, although I am uncertain which individual vehicle is which.

CHAPTER 11

Tramcars

During the latter part of the nineteenth century and the early years of the twentieth century, travelling by tram through the streets of the vast majority of towns and cities was the only way to get about for most people, as motor cars were still very much in their infancy at that time.

Several of the larger cities began operating horse-drawn trams. In time, the horse-drawn trams were replaced with steam trams, and then with electric ones, although there were some instances where the operating tram company felt that business was dwindling and they discontinued the tram service altogether, removed the tracks and scrapped their vehicles.

In the course of time, however, the motor car and omnibus became the more popular mode of transport for getting about. As they were not restricted – considering that the majority of tram systems very rarely went beyond the boundaries of the towns and cities that they operated in – business dropped off and tramway systems were closed.

Some of the tramway systems did survive, however, with the overhead wires being kept in situ, but the tracks were removed and the tramcars were subsequently replaced by trolleybuses. Then, as bus operating companies became bigger and began to travel further afield out of the towns and cities, the days of the trolleybuses themselves soon became numbered.

When the tramway systems closed, several of the bodies of those companies' tramcars were offered for sale, including the double-deck cars – where the upper and lower saloons were usually sold as separate items. The vast majority of these bodies were bought by farmers who used them as coops for their ducks, geese or chickens. Many have now been long scrapped, but there are still a few dotted about, with new discoveries still occurring today.

A good number of these bodies have since been recovered and restored or are awaiting restoration. The National Tramway Museum & Village at Crich in Derbyshire has been successful in trying to preserve as many of these tramcar bodies as possible (*see Chapter 19*).

Operating in Northern Ireland between 1885 and 1948 was the narrow gauge hydro-electrically powered passenger and freight Bessbrook & Newry Tramway. Power was originally provided by two motor carriages and two more were built at a later date. The tramway had a number of goods wagons and two brake vans, and there was one closed passenger trailer, although in time three more and an open one were added. The wheels on the wagons were flangeless, which would enable them to be pulled along the roads by horses (later by tractors). A set of rails were fitted to the outside of the tram tracks and were about 7/8 of an inch shorter. The wheels of the wagons would run along this second set of rails, with the taller tram tracks acting as a guide. These wagons were always carried in between a motor carriage and a passenger trailer, with the brake van bringing up the rear.

When the line closed in January 1948, all the stock was sold to George Cohen & Sons (scrap merchants) at Sydenham in Belfast. Built in 1922 by the Starbuck Company in Birkenhead, Merseyside, this closed passenger trailer, No. 6, had a seating capacity of twelve. Its body was purchased by the sisters at the Convent of Mercy in Bessbrook and it was placed at the front of the convent grounds, where it was used as a summer house with an absolutely splendid view across the valley (with the Newry Viaduct visible in the distance). It was pictured here on 8 April 2015. However, since my visit the body has been removed to the headquarters of the Railway Preservation Society of Ireland at Whitehead to be completely restored.

The Bournemouth Corporation Tramway's line ran the 16 miles between Bournemouth and Poole. Operating from 1902 until 1936, it used a fleet of one single-deck and 151 double-deck tram cars. Considering the line closed some eighty-two years ago, a substantial number of vehicle bodies still survive to this day. This example, No. 113, was built in 1924 by Brush at Loughborough and was the first out of a batch of twenty built between then and 1926.

Following closure of the tramway, this body ended up as a chicken coop on a farm in Milton Abbas in Dorset. In 2014, Richard Lee, the co-founder and owner of Plankbridge Hutmakers – who specialise in making and restoring shepherds' huts – was visiting the farm after the owner requested a quote to repair two huts that he owned. He spotted the now severely derelict-looking tramcar body and purchased it from the farmer. It was then transported to his company's premises near Piddlehinton, where it was restored and used as an office and design studio. Upon visiting the site on 28 March 2017, I took this picture of it in use.

This 1903-built single-decker tramcar was photographed at the East Anglia Transport Museum at Carlton Colville in Suffolk on 12 August 2007. It was built for the Lowestoft Corporation Tramways by G. F. Milnes & Co. at Hadley Castle in Shropshire, and was one of four such built. The units were numbered from 20 to 23, and at the time of writing it is presently not known which one this example actually is. When the tramway closed in 1931, this vehicle was sold and had a bungalow built around it. In 1988, the bungalow came up for sale and the body, which nobody knew anything about at the time, was purchased by the East Anglia Transport Trust, being moved to their site at Carlton Colville, where it is currently being used as a small objects museum.

Founded in 1901 and running until 1950 was the 51-mile Newcastle Corporation Tramway. The tramway operated a fleet of twenty double-deck open-topped tramcars, which were built in 1901 by Hurst Nelson & Co. in Motherwell, Scotland. This car, No. 117, was one of those twenty. Following the closure of the tramway, this lower saloon body, plus five others (one other Newcastle and four Sheffield Corporation ones), were all purchased from Brigg Market in 1951 for £25 each. Taken to Susworth in Lincolnshire, they were separated and used as chicken coops, workshops and holiday lets. Photographed on 15 October 2017, at the same location it was taken to some sixty-six years earlier, No. 117, which was formerly used as a workshop, was seen looking the worse for wear, its better and happier days behind it.

One of the six bodies purchased, as described in the previous caption, was No. 446, a lower saloon from an enclosed double-decker tram. It was built in 1924 by the Sheffield Corporation Tramway at their Tinsley Depot, just outside of Sheffield, and was one of the 884 trams that this corporation operated from 1873 to 1960 over its 48 miles of track. Photographed on 15 October 2017, it was still being used as a workshop. Note the purpose-built wooden shutters for the windows, which not only protect them, but can also be removed to let the light in, as the shuttered side faces towards the sun. Sadly, one window pane has been accidentally cracked, as can be seen to the left of the door. Apart from that, the vehicle is in excellent condition.

Between 1878 and 1937 the Swansea Improvements & Tramway Company operated trams over 13 miles of track in and around Swansea. When the tramway closed, however, it was not all doom and gloom for the Welsh city, as the Swansea & Mumbles Railway continued to operate for another twenty-three years, until 1960. Built in 1924 by the Brush Electrical Engineering Company at Loughborough, in Leicestershire, as a lowbridge double-decker tramcar, this example was one of a batch of thirteen. Sadly, at the time of writing its exact identity is unknown. It was sold following the closure of the tramway and was transported to Brynamman, in the Black Mountains, where it was used as a chicken coop until the mid-1980s.

At the time of my visit there on 7 April 1999, it had lain unused for numerous years and was in a semi-derelict condition, although the actual body framework was still in pretty good shape. At the tail end of 2015 it had been rescued by members of the Amman Valley Railway Society and removed from the location in which it had been sat for seventy-eight years, where it was exposed to the harsh elements found in that part of Wales. They are hoping to restore it back to its former glory.

CHAPTER 12

Pre-Grouping Freight Stock Vehicles

Companies Amalgamated into the Great Western Railway (GWR)

There are literally thousands of freight wagon bodies that are being used throughout the country as sheds and animal shelters, etc. As the with NPCCS vehicles from the constituent companies, I haven't found a single body of any freight vehicle that originated with those companies. There are numerous examples that came from the GWR during the pre-Grouping era though, which is hardly surprising when you take into consideration that in 1902 the GWR had 59,036 freight vehicles on its books. What is surprising is that in 1926 they owned some 88,590, so it can only be assumed that the majority of these additional 29,500 or so vehicles were in fact newly built after 1923.

Although not strictly built by an amalgamated company, this vehicle was built by the Great Western Railway during the pre-Grouping era. Constructed at Swindon in 1897 as part of a batch of 100, this was 10-ton four-wheeled 'Iron-Mink' No. 59260. These wagons were built for the conveying of gunpowder – hence the body being constructed of iron instead of wood. It should be noted that the wooden framing around the doors is only attached to the outside by about a dozen or so nails and is an original feature. Seeing out its days as a storage shed on a farm, this 100-year-old veteran was pictured on 25 May 1997 at Wroughton in Wiltshire, where it had lain for over half its life, having been purchased in 1965. Traces of rusting can be seen on the lower part of the doors and on the nearest corner.

Companies Amalgamated into the London, Midland & Scottish Railway (LMS)

As has been already stated, the LMS was the largest company from the Big Four, and after Grouping they owned 291,490 freight vehicles. Therefore, it is hardly surprising to find that a large proportion of freight vehicle bodies from the constituent companies have survived, finding themselves being used for animal shelters or store sheds, to name but two examples.

Pictured at Manafon in Powys on 19 April 2003 while in use as a store shed was this rather unique vehicle, which was numbered 142350 by the LMS in 1923. It originated with the Lancashire & Yorkshire Railway and its history is unknown, though it was probably built at their Newton Heath works in Manchester during the early twentieth century.

A few factors make this quite a rare vehicle. Firstly, it would seem that it started life as a five-plank open goods wagon; this can be determined from the diagonal metal bracing strips from the bottom of the door, which finish at the top of the fifth plank from the bottom. Secondly, it has at some point in time then been converted to a non-ventilated covered goods wagon, by building the sides up and adding a sliding door and a roof. Thirdly, the metal edges on the upper corners are not seen on any other L&YR covered goods wagons and have been added to match those on the lower five planks. Lastly, the planks above the five bottom ones are much narrower and the cross bracing seen on the door appeared on the sides as well in other covered goods wagons built by the L&YR. All of these factors mark this vehicle as an oddity, which makes you wonder if it was built specifically for a special purpose. There are currently no photographs that I have found of other vehicles that look anything like this example.

This vehicle, No. 26981, started life in approximately 1917 as a four-wheeled non-ventilated tranship van, and was built for the LNWR at their Earlestown works. Tranship vans were originally goods wagons that were built with a canvas top above the doors, which rolled back to the centre of the vehicle for the ease of loading and unloading of certain goods (sacks of grain, wheat or salt, etc.).

Several of these vehicles were withdrawn from service in 1959/60 and many of them were sold to either the Army or Navy, or to Port Authorities across the country. This example (re-numbered 126981 by the LMS in 1923) was used by the Port of Bristol Authority and was numbered in their number series as 1455. From the early 1970s until the mid-1980s, the authority sold off their railway freight wagons, many of which were purchased by preservation societies. This example, however, was one of a dozen or so bodies that were purchased from a scrap dealer by a farmer, being taken to his farm in Bradford Leigh, in Wiltshire, for use as pigsties, storage sheds and, as demonstrated by this picture taken on 2 February 2008, as stables or animal shelters.

The use of freight vehicle bodies can be just as varied as coaches and tramcars, as can be seen in this picture taken on 21 June 1997 at Bishops Frome in Herefordshire. It shows the body of a 1912-built Midland Railway four-wheeled, eight-planked open coke wagon, which was numbered 104620. Following its purchase in the 1960s, its wheels and running gear were removed and it was turned upside down for use as an animal shelter, along with the identical vehicle beside.

Companies Amalgamated into the London & North Eastern Railway (LNER)

Despite being the second-largest company of the Big Four, the LNER surprisingly had the smallest amount of freight wagons, totalling a meagre 29,700. Bodies from the constituent companies that became part of the LNER are therefore not very high in numbers, although wagons built by the LNER are fairly well represented as grounded bodies.

Built at Stratford works for the Great Eastern Railway in about 1920, this 10-ton, four-wheeled, ventilated goods van was numbered 25206. It was re-numbered 625206 by the LNER after Grouping in 1923 and was withdrawn from service in the late 1960s. It was then bought by a farmer and taken to a field near Shirebrook, Nottinghamshire, where it was pictured on 4 May 1997 as an out of use cattle shelter. Note the remains of wooden covers on the ends, which would have hidden the now exposed ventilators.

This unidentified vehicle is a Great North of Scotland Railway 10-ton, four-wheeled, ventilated covered goods wagon which was probably built around 1920 at the railway's works in Inverurie, Aberdeenshire. Upon its withdrawal from service in 1962, the body was purchased and transported to Crimongorth in Aberdeenshire, where one end was removed and replaced with twin doors for use as a garage. However, at the time of my visit on 27 March 2016 it had been moved from its original position, and was in use as a general rubbish store. Following its move, one end of the vehicle began to collapse, as can be seen in the picture, so it is unlikely to survive another move.

Companies Amalgamated into the Southern Railway (SR)

As with the other three companies, the bodies of freight wagons from the pre-Grouping era companies that formed part of the SR are very difficult to come across, which is hardly surprising as the railway only owned 37,500 freight wagons in total. Having said that, one or two vehicles from that period have been found.

The Isle of Wight Railway was the first to appear on the island, being formed in 1860. Only three freight vehicles are known to have survived from this railway, of which this is one. Built in 1912 as a 10-ton, four-wheeled, non-ventilated goods wagon and numbered 61 (later becoming No. 87), like all surviving vehicles at Grouping it was transferred into the ownership of the Southern Railway and was allocated the number 46979 (although it appears that this was never carried). It was withdrawn in 1927 and became an animal shelter on the island before being saved by the Isle of Wight Steam Railway. Taken to their base at Havenstreet, it was photographed awaiting restoration there on 12 February 2000.

In 1880 the Freshwater, Yarmouth & Newport Railway was formed on the Isle of Wight and began running freight services, which were operated by the Isle of Wight Railway. It would be another nine years before they ran passenger services, which were operated by the Isle of Wight Central Railway. In 1913 the FY&NR decided to break away from the other two and go it alone in running their own railway. They purchased a small number of secondhand vehicles from the two companies in order to do this and one of them can be seen being used as an ice cream kiosk on the beach at the Duver at St Helens, where it was seen on 12 February 2000 (although it was closed for the winter). This vehicle originated in the LB&SCR in the 1880s as a 10-ton, four-wheeled goods brake van; in 1907 it was acquired by the IWCR (its original and IWCR numbers are not known) and following its purchase by the FY&NR it became No. 13 in their fleet; in 1923 the SR re-numbered it to 56038. It was to remain in service on the island until 1966, when it was withdrawn and its body was sold and transported to where it was pictured.

CHAPTER 13

Post-Grouping Freight
Stock Vehicles

Great Western Railway (GWR)

As stated in the previous chapter, while some bodies built by the Great Western Railway before Grouping still exist, several hundred vehicles built after 1923 can found dotted around the country.

Located on the platform of the Old Station in Blagdon, North Somerset, is this former GWR 20-ton, four-wheeled goods brake van, No. 17955, which was built in Swindon in 1922. It is currently used as a summer house, having been purchased during the mid-1980s.

The GWR gave all their vehicles a telegraphic code name as they were a very meticulous company, even to the extent of fitting plates to their stock which read 'Please return to the Great Western Railway as soon as possible'. All GWR vehicles were closely scrutinised by the company and records were sent every day by telegraph by every stationmaster to district offices, so the whereabouts of every vehicle could be traced. Goods brake vans such as this example were given the code name of 'Toad'. Just like their passenger and non-carrying stock, GWR freight vehicles all had their numbers stamped into the underframe (usually beneath where the builder's plate would be attached). If they had not done this then I would not have been able to identify this vehicle.

Some freight vehicles are often confused with non-passenger-carrying coaching stock and the ventilated 'Mink G' vans are one such type. This is mainly due to them having two sets of twin doors on each side (similar to fruit or fish vans). This unidentified example was built around 1931 and was numbered in the 112xxx series. It was pictured on 23 May 1999 on a farm at Llanspyddid in Powys, where it was out of use as an animal shelter, but it was originally used as a shed for lambing when purchased in 1962.

Another type of vehicle confused for non-passenger-carrying coaching stock was the 33-feet-long motor car van, given the telegraphic code name of 'Asmo'. They are similar to covered carriage trucks in having a set of ventilated double doors on each end; the difference between them was that these vehicles also had a set of double doors in the centre of each side. Situated beneath the end doors was a metal flap, which would be dropped down level with the loading bay before the vehicles were driven inside, where they were secured with ropes to tethering rings. The side doors meant that the vehicles could be accessed from a station platform in order to check the condition of the vehicles and ensure that they were still tightly tethered, thus eliminating the need to open the end doors.

This example, No. 116934, was built in 1930 and was one of a batch of twenty-five vehicle bodies of various types purchased from Woodham's yard in Barry and from Castleton Turf in Wentlooge in the ten-year period between 1962 and 1972. These bodies were used as animal shelters, calving and lambing sheds and as feed stores. This particular one was used to store two vintage horse-drawn dray wagons and was pictured on the old coast road between Newport and Cardiff at St Brides on 20 December 1998.

In the early 1950s, some GWR ventilated goods vans were re-built by British Railways into experimental pallet vans in order to gauge their effectiveness, prior to BR deciding whether to build to their own design on a much larger scale. This rebuilding involved removing the sides and replacing them with a set of two heavy cupboard-style doors on each side at the left-hand end. The right-hand end would consist of additional metal diagonal bracing for added strength. These vehicles enabled whole pallets to be loaded into the vehicles from each side simultaneously. This experiment proved to be a success, so BR built several of their own, with the major differences being the standard ventilated corrugated steel ends, while the bodywork was made of plywood.

Built at Swindon works in around 1927, No. 114383 was one of those converted vans. It was found languishing in a field at Purton in Wiltshire on 2 June 2012, where, despite still being in very good condition, it was out of use as an animal shelter.

London, Midland & Scottish Railway (LMS)

The largest of the four companies quite possibly has the largest number of bodies that can be found; though it is probably a close call between them and the GWR as to who has the most numbers of grounded bodies still extant, I personally feel that the LMS might just edge it. Like the GWR, the total runs into the many hundreds.

Situated at Taw Bridge Cross in Devon, and clearly visible perched high upon two breeze block walls, are two 12-foot ventilated goods vans. Used as a grain store and an animal pellet feed store, they are part of a collection of four. The other two – out of shot on the left of the picture, but mounted onto concrete pillars at ground level – were used as general store sheds. These four vehicles comprised two LMSR and two LNER vans and they were purchased from Barnstaple station in the 1960s.

The two pictured here are No. 147471 on the left of the picture, which, built in about 1935, comes from the Wolverton works of the LMSR, and the one on the right is No. 246007, which was built by the LNER at Darlington in about 1940. No. 147471 housed the sacks of animal feed pellets while No. 246007 housed the sacks of grain. Both vehicles were out of use when photographed on 1 October 2015; however, this was not the case when I first visited in November 1999. Note how these vehicles are located at such a height as to keep the rats from getting at the grain. Also note how both vehicles still retain their solebars (complete with builders' plates – as do the other two vehicles), and it can clearly be defined where the buffers and couplings would have been situated.

The LMSR had 1,000 steel-bodied goods vans built during 1929/30. However, unlike the GWR 'Iron Mink' (featured in the last chapter), these vehicles were not used for the transportation of gunpowder as the company had specially designed different vehicles constructed for that purpose. These 1,000 vehicles were built by four different builders to LMS designs, although it must be stated that there were differences; for instance, some of the vans were built with metal cross bracings on the doors, while others had just plain doors. This example, No. 179998, was one of the former. Pictured on 21 November 2009 on the Great Central Railway in Loughborough, it was in use as a store shed.

As mentioned previously, the LMS had specially designed vehicles for the transportation of gunpowder. These were non-ventilated and had a set of two steel cupboard doors on each side (instead of the sliding door). This example, No. 213067, was built at Earlestown in 1929 and following its withdrawal from revenue-earning service it was taken into departmental stock. Having a hole cut in each end with a sliding cover, its departmental use was as a track observation vehicle (hence the holes). It was pictured at Causey Arch Level Crossing on the Tanfield Railway in County Durham on 8 July 2003, where it is used as a tea and snack van, with the holes acting as serving hatches.

Built at Wolverton in approximately 1927, this four-wheeled ventilated goods van was No. 309982. Like many other vans it was taken into departmental use and altered in some way to reflect its new purpose; in this case, the ventilators on each end were removed and a door was fitted between the vertical metal stanchions on both ends. The reason for this alteration was to allow the vehicle to be used as a mobile workshop on electric trains, and it could be coupled between coaches with corridor connections to allow safe working while carrying out maintenance or installing overhead lines. Upon its final withdrawal from service, its body was placed next to Upper Poppleton station in York, where it was pictured on 6 April 2012. Here it was used as a storage shed for the permanent way department, as can be evidenced by the piles of concrete sleepers around it.

This 20-ton goods brake van was built at Derby works in 1927 and was numbered 357924. Its body was pictured on 7 April 2007 with a magnificent backdrop at Blaenau Ffestiniog, Gwynedd, where it was being used as a workshop. If the vehicle's number is missing from the exterior, it can often be found on the inside of the guard's lookout duckets. Note the monorail track and wagons in the foreground. These are part of the biggest single collection of locomotives, coaches and wagons of this unusual gauge in the entire British Isles, and possibly the world. They can now be observed at the Tanat Valley Light Railway near Nantmawr in Shropshire, along with the brake van body, both having been moved there during 2016/17.

One of the last type of vehicles built by the LMS was a plywood-bodied goods van which had the sliding door that the LMSR used on 90 per cent of the goods vans they built between 1923 and Nationalisation in 1948. This example, No. 522230, was built in 1944 and was seen being used as a general store shed on a farm near Buckland St Mary in Somerset on 16 September 1995. As can be seen, the biggest problem with these types of vans was the doors, which were forever being replaced due to the bearings going, causing the door to drop out of its runners.

London & North Eastern Railway (LNER)

Given that this company had the least number of freight wagons out of the four, it is surprising to find that the number of surviving bodies from this company is more than double that from the Southern Railway, who had some 7,800 more vehicles.

Like the LMS, the LNER also favoured building their covered goods vans with a single sliding door on each side and they built them in abundance. These types of vehicle replaced the similar-looking North Eastern Railway goods vans that were acquired at the grouping and they would have either a steel or wooden underframe. This example, numbered 138709, was built in 1930 and has a wooden underframe. It was pictured on 19 April 1997 at Stoke Works Junction, near Bromsgrove, being used as a shed on an allotment, complete with a 'Private Land' notice attached to the external louvred sliding ventilator on the vehicle's end.

The LNER converted 1,200 vans to fruit vans at their York works during 1935/36. This was done by removing the shutters from the ends and replacing the lower half of the ends with louvred planking, roof ventilators and a large cast metal plate reading the word 'FRUIT' on the door. This unidentified example was one of those converted vans and was found on a farm in Herefordshire on 7 June 1997, where as you can see the roof ventilators have been removed and the roof re-felted. Apart from the door, it appears to be in very good condition, serving as a store for bags of cement, which are just visible inside the door.

By 1934 the LNER had decided to follow the LMS and began building goods vans with the now familiar corrugated steel ends. Built in 1936 was this example, which as you can clearly see is of the non-ventilated variety, but it still has the two small corrugations. This one was being used as a store for a local football club in St Blazey, Cornwall, and was photographed securely locked up on 9 May 1997. Note the church tower in the background. This vehicle was scrapped in around 2005 and was replaced by a new purpose-built brick structure.

One of the last types of goods vans built by the LNER was the design shown here. They were made from either vertical matchboard or, as in this example, plywood. Some of these vehicles were converted to fruit vans at Darlington works, with the lower half of the ends being replaced with louvres, but the end ventilators would remain in place. This example, No. 261773, was built in 1943 at Darlington and was purchased from Woodham's yard in about 1972. It was then transported near to Llandovery in Carmarthenshire, where one end was cut away and it was used as a garage for the family's car. However, at the time of my visit on 25 April 1998, the elderly couple that owned it were sadly no longer able to drive, so the body was turned into a wood and log store.

Southern Railway (SR)

Freight vehicle bodies from this railway are the least commonly found from the Big Four; in fact, there are probably more non-passenger-carrying bodies from this company to be found than there are freight wagons.

Although numerous in total, the covered goods vans that were built by the Southern Railway were uniform in design, with the only real differences being with the material that they were made of. Built at Ashford Works in Kent in 1943, this plywood-bodied version, No. 50942, was withdrawn during the early years of the 1970s and was purchased by a farmer from Rooks Bridge in Somerset from Woodham Brothers scrapyard in Barry along with half a dozen other bodies. On 25 April 1996 it was pictured on a sunny day, being used as a stable for two ponies.

This rather splendid-looking potting shed, complete with its hanging baskets of flowers, began life at Ashford Works in 1938 as an insulated banana van, No. 50818, for the Southern Railway. It is identical to the previous image, except there are no ventilators on the ends and the body is planked. These vehicles were heavier than the other goods vans built by the SR, due to the layer of insulation and internally fitted steam heating equipment (which was used to keep the fruit from deteriorating too quickly while in transit). This example was pictured on the Old Coast Road between Newport and Cardiff, at the village of Nash, on 13 September 1997.

CHAPTER 14

Irish Railways Freight Stock Vehicles

Unlike on the mainland, where you can see many hundreds of bodies being used for various purposes in almost any part of the country, the fields in the Irish countryside are virtually devoid of these freight vehicle bodies. In fact, I have only come across a small handful of locations where bodies have existed. In part, this is due to the Irish railways having very few freight wagons. Having said this, I have recently come across a forum in which people give locations of where these freight vehicles can still be found in use in Ireland, and they are more numerous than I had first thought.

The numbers of surviving freight vehicles from Irish railway companies are nowhere close to matching the amount found on the mainland. This unidentified example is a Great Northern Railway of Ireland covered goods van, which was pictured on 4 April 2015 in the yard at Downpatrick, at the base of the Downpatrick & County Down Heritage Railway, where it was being used as a general store shed. This vehicle was donated to the railway by the widow of a local man, who purchased it in the early 1960s and used it as a workshop in his garden. Note the wooden fencing panels that cover the sides and ends of the vehicle; these were applied after the local council insisted that the body be made more appealing to the eye, following a couple of complaints from the man's neighbours that the van was an eyesore.

One of the more unusual vehicles comes in the form of this former Cavan & Leitrim Railway 'Shawlie' wagon, which was undergoing restoration by members of the Belturbet Railway & Vintage Restoration Association at their museum in Belturbet when seen on 28 April 2011. The C&LR was a narrow gauge railway that ran from 1887 until 1959. It comprised a 34-mile main line between Dromod and Belturbet and a 15-mile branch line between Ballinamore and Arigna.

This wagon could be converted to carry either general goods or cattle depending upon the requirement. It was rescued in a badly dilapidated condition in early 2011 from a field where it had lain since 1960, being used as a cattle shelter. Due to the condition of the vehicle, it was lifted very gingerly by four tractors onto a road trailer chassis (hence the road wheels), the whole process taking just over five hours. It was then taken to the association's site, where it was propped up by six beer kegs to await restoration.

Also pictured on 28 April 2011 at the same location as the previous image were the rather dilapidated bodies of these two Córas Iompair Éireann (Irish Rail) plywood-bodied goods vans. Built during the 1950s or '60s, they were rescued from a farm with the prospect of possibly being restored. The difference between the quality of materials that were used to build the 'Shawlie' wagon and these two is clearly evident, given that the former lay in a field open to the elements for over fifty years and this pair were only withdrawn from service in the mid-1980s, and that was with these being built at a much later date.

CHAPTER 15

Private Owner Freight Stock Vehicles

During the Second World War, the Railway Executive Committee were responsible for overseeing operations on Britain's railway network. There were some 500,000 freight wagons under their control, with a vast percentage of those belonging to companies who owned quarries or coal mines. The bodies of these earlier private owner wagons are very hard to find. However, there are several examples to be found at preserved heritage railways and in the odd museum here and there. These wagons, although privately owned, were permitted to run on the mainline and the situation is the same nowadays, with wagons owned by private companies found operating across the entire rail network.

Constructed between 1974 and 1978 by W. H. Davis at Langwith Junction in Derbyshire as part of a batch of 300, these two-axle mineral hopper wagons were built onto the underframes of redundant tank wagons. This example, No. 24312, was pictured on 27 August 2000 at the Appleby Frodingham Railway Preservation Society, which is located within the grounds of the Scunthorpe Steelworks. It has had most of one side removed and is being used as a coal bunker for use in the society's steam locomotive.

The Port of Bristol Authority operated many vehicles, such as goods vans, open-planked wagons and grain vans, many of which were second-hand and purchased from numerous pre-Grouping companies. They also had their own numbering scheme, separated into vehicle type. This example, numbered 775 under the authority's numbering scheme, was one of their four-wheeled grain vans. Little information is known about this vehicle other than that it was purchased in the 1970s or 1980s as part of a batch of a dozen or so, and was taken to Bradford Leigh in Wiltshire to be used as an animal shelter. However, when seen on 2 February 2008 it was looking rather forlorn, its users having abandoned it some time ago. The tree growing out of its roof and door bear testament to this – although the hoof prints in the mud around the door seem to offer a different view.

A popular sight on Britain's railways during the 1950s and '60s were the apex-roofed Saxa Salt vans, with their distinguishable all-over yellow livery and branding. Seen on 1 April 2013 at the Waverley Route Heritage Association base at Whitrope in the Scottish Borders was this unidentified example, which was being used as a store shed. With its yellow paintwork faded and peeling, but retaining its 'Saxa Salt' branding, it keeps company with an LNER goods van body.

CHAPTER 16

British Railways Freight Stock Vehicles

Following the end of the Second World War, the Labour Government under Prime Minister Clement Attlee decided the railways of the country would be nationalised, which led to the Transport Act of 1947. On 1 January 1948 the four companies formed at the grouping in 1923 were taken over by the Railway Executive of the British Transport Commission, with all rolling stock and infrastructure coming under the umbrella of a new business named British Railways (BR). During the early 1950s BR began building rolling stock to their own designs, thereby making a huge amount of the stock acquired from the Big Four surplus to requirements, which led to them being disposed of and subsequently scrapped. Following the cuts instigated by Dr Richard Beeching in 1966, BR found their works, yards and sidings overwhelmed with redundant items of rolling stock and again BR were faced with disposing of these items of stock. Several thousand of them were sold to scrap merchants throughout the country. One of these merchants was Dai Woodham, who had a scrapyard in Barry, South Wales, which later became famous for its rows of steam locomotives, as Dai refused to scrap them, which led to the majority of them being preserved at heritage railways and museums and has also seen a few return to running on the main line again. The general public could purchase from Dai (and many other merchants) the bodies of freight wagons to use however they wished to. The vehicles that were purchased from Woodham's yard were easily distinguished from other merchants' because when they were bought from BR, they had a large painted letter 'W' in yellow paint applied to their body sides and many can still be found with these on them.

In the opening chapter of this book can be found the body of a Cambrian Railways observation saloon which, as stated, was moved for preservation and restoration. As part of the agreement, the body of another vehicle would replace it; this is that vehicle, which was seen on 12 December 2007. It was built by the Birmingham Railway Carriage & Wagon Company in 1957 as a 20-ton plough ballast brake van (so called because there was a snow plough affixed to both ends beneath the solebar). It was numbered in the engineers' fleet series as DB 993800 and was withdrawn in the 1990s. At the time of writing it has been converted into luxurious glamping accommodation in the Somerset countryside (complete with double bed, shower, toilet and dining room).

Following a dispute in the 1960s between BR, ASLEF and the National Union of Railwaymen regarding train guards riding in the rear cabs of the locomotives that were hauling the 'Freightliner' concept trains that had recently been introduced, these caboose wagons were introduced in 1965. They were placed onto flat wagons at the rear of the consist but they were short-lived, being withdrawn later in the same year. There were two main reasons for their demise: the first one was due to the poor ride quality, with numerous guards suffering injuries as a result of being thrown around inside of them like a rag-doll; the second reason was that the 'goldfish bowl' style of the lookouts on the sides tended to distort the guard's view of the train, especially while in motion. This example, numbered 99Z03, was pictured on 8 April 2012 being used as a security cabin at the Newbridge permanent way depot on the heritage North Yorkshire Moors Railway.

Built in 1957 by the Pressed Steel Company Ltd at their Linwood Works in Renfrewshire (about 14 miles west of Glasgow), this vehicle was just one of the 206,000 plus of this type that were built. It started life as a 16-ton, welded-body, end-door mineral wagon, one of the most numerous type of freight wagon that British Railways ever built. It was photographed on 28 April 1996 within the yard of C. F. Booth's at Rotherham in South Yorkshire, where it was keeping company with another similar body. There were a few others also dotted around the site, all of which had a large hole cut into one side of them and were being used as containers to keep separated scrap parts in. Having being sold by BR as scrap upon their withdrawal, their bodies were thus re-used by the scrap firm who bought them in order to keep their yard as tidy as possible.

On 1 January 1948, when the railways were nationalised, BR decided that all the rolling stock that had been acquired (which included the 1.2 million freight wagons) would be given a prefix letter to their running numbers, to denote which of the previous four companies each one had been inherited from. The letters applied were: 'W' for ex-GWR, 'M' for ex-LMS, 'E' for ex-LNER and 'S' for ex-SR vehicles. The same letters would be applied at a later date to the carriages and NPCCS vehicles that were built by BR, to denote that those vehicles were allocated to a certain area or region: W – Western, M – Midland, E – Eastern, S – Southern. The letters Sc were also applied to vehicles in the Scottish Region. BR started building vehicles to their own design in the early 1950s and those were given the prefix letter of 'B'. Among the most numerous types of vehicles built by BR were the 12-ton covered goods vans. This example, No. B 757733, was an all plank-bodied version that was built in 1951 at Wolverton Works in Buckinghamshire. It was pictured being used as a store shed on 21 April 2000 at Latcham in Somerset. Note the yellow painted 'W' on its side, denoting that it came from Dai Woodham's scrapyard in Barry.

Seen in use as a store shed alongside the Midland Railway Centre at Swanwick Junction in Derbyshire on 16 September 2017, this 1962 Derby works-built plywood van was No. B784127. It is instantly noticeable how different it is from the previous example: the doors are on roller channels (as opposed to being hinged) and they slide open towards the ends of the body. These vehicles were known as 'vanwides' and were designed for the carriage of complete wooden pallets and so that they would be able to be unloaded at stations with narrower platforms than usual. All of them were built of plywood. A good number of them were converted from being vacuum-braked to air-braked and saw use on the Speedfreight/link rail services until their demise during the late 1980s/early 1990s. The MOD also purchased vast numbers of these air-braked conversions for use at their supply depots and other sites across the country.

Although this vehicle looks like any other 12-ton goods van, it is actually a shock absorbing van, built to prevent breakages of fragile goods such as glassware and pottery. It differs from other goods vans as the body is 6 inches shorter than the underframe, which was achieved by making the section either side of the doors narrower than on the standard vans (as can be clearly seen). Underneath the doors was a large spring wrapped around a metal bar, so that when the train stopped the body would rock from side to side along the underframe instead of jolting to a halt. The white stripes were applied to the sides and ends of these vehicles following an increase in accidents during shunting when fingers and hands would become trapped when the body moved; this was so that yard shunters would know to keep clear of these vehicles. This example (No. B 852219) was pictured on a farm at Othery on the Somerset Levels on 17 July 1995.

This rather unique specimen is a 10-ton ventilated meat van, and it was used for the transportation of fresh meat across the country. It was built at Wolverton works in 1952 and was numbered B870036. As you can see, it looks like any other goods van, except it has four ventilators in a vertical column on each end. This was to maximise air circulating within the van while the meat was being conveyed. Note the shunter board on the end, adjacent to the bottom ventilator. These boards were also found on the sides of vehicles, although this example, seen being used as a general junk store at East Keal in Lincolnshire on 5 May 1997, appears to be missing them. Several of these vehicles were later converted to convey ale, and this example was one of them. This is apparent as the side panels were originally fitted with louvres, but they have been replaced on this vehicle by planks.

This vehicle is a plywood-bodied, 12-ton insulated banana van, built in 1959 and numbered B 882187. It was pictured on 4 April 1997 being used as a workshop (complete with electricity supply to power the tools and lighting inside) at Clawton in North Devon. The main difference between this vehicle and other goods vans is the lack of hooded ventilators on the ends. This, combined with the heavy insulation on the inside of the vehicle, was to prevent the fruit within going black before reaching the shelves in the shops.

BR built pallet vans that used the same mechanism as the shock-absorbing vans covered earlier. This vehicle, pictured on 21 November 2009 at Loughborough on the Great Central Railway, was clearly one of those examples; indeed, the three vertical stripes on the side give that away. The external bracing on the right-hand side of this example, No. B855667 (built at Wolverton in 1961) is made of flat pieces of metal stanchions that are not so heavy-duty, allowing the large sliding door to open along the grooved channels in the top and bottom of the vehicle. The door, with its wooden 'nine squares effect', is also another giveaway of the origins of these vehicles, which were known as 'palshocvans'.

The last vehicle that I shall feature in this chapter is one that is very rare to find, with only a couple of examples having been preserved. Those vehicles are cattle wagons, which didn't have the corrugated steel ends & hooded ventilators but were loosely based on the GWR goods van design. The top part of the body was open with a single horizontal bar across it; there were two 'stable-style' doors with a drop-down flap, which formed a ramp to be able to load and unload the animals more easily. This example, No. B 893407, was built in 1951 at Swindon as an 8-ton version (later, 10-ton versions were introduced) and was purchased from a scrapyard in the 1960s – having seen a very short working life – and was used as a cattle shed originally, but at the time of my visit to Killamarsh in Derbyshire on 30 August 1998, it was being used to house sheep and goats.

CHAPTER 17

Post-Grouping Lift On/Off Container Stock

Lift on/off containers started appearing on the railways after the grouping in 1923. They were simply van bodies of various sizes with lifting eyes attached to the top, so that they could be transferred from a road vehicle into a wagon and vice-versa upon reaching their destination. They were carried inside of an open wagon and securely tethered by either ropes or chains, depending on what was available where they were loaded. Each of the four companies built containers to their own design and although they were similar there was no uniformity for each type; this all changed in the late 1930s when the Railway Clearing House (RCH) became responsible for their design and issued a 'standard' design for each type which had to be strictly adhered to by the companies.

Great Western Railway (GWR)

With the transportation of containers increasing, the railway companies introduced wagons specifically built for this purpose. The GWR was the first of the four to introduce the 'conflat' wagon idea. These were basically a flat wagon with no sides but with chains fitted to secure the containers to them. Vehicles from the GWR and the other three companies are quite rare to find, but some do exist.

Of all the different types of containers built, the most numerous were the BD general-purpose containers which were used for carrying a variety of things ranging from foodstuffs to clothing and electrical goods. They had a pair of stable doors on one end with a drop-down flap and a pair of doors on both sides. This example, numbered BD 2478W (the suffix letter would denote which company built it), was being used as an animal shelter when it was pictured during a heavy snowstorm on 13 April 1998 at Old Sodbury in Gloucestershire.

London, Midland & Scottish Railway (LMS)

At first, the LMS took to utilising other freight wagons for the purpose of transporting their container stock, with the main source of these vehicles being the underframes from their fleet of four-wheeled milk tanks. Eventually they built specially designed wagons, but their wagons did not have any floors and were called 'chassis' wagons. These wagons were allocated a specific code depending on the type of container they would carry. More of these vehicles survived from this railway than the others, which is hardly surprising, seeing how it was the largest.

This shed doing sturdy work at Stoke Works Junction allotments near Bromsgrove began its working life at Wolverton works in Buckinghamshire in the late 1920s or early 1930s as an LMS A type container (which were the smallest of all containers). It was given the number of A 53M. These containers would have carried crates of small items such as buttons, nuts, bolts, screws, etc. or even confectionary. This example, pictured on 19 April 1997 surrounded by clutter, was withdrawn from service in the mid-1960s.

London & North Eastern Railway (LNER)

Before developing its own container-carrying wagons, the LNER used some of its cattle wagons with all the bodywork removed. Like the GWR, their specially built wagons had floors and were therefore classified as 'conflats'. Once again, a few of these can still be found on farms and the like today.

No. FM637E was built at Darlington works in 1937 by the LNER as a 14-foot 12-inch-long plywood-bodied insulated fresh meat container (hence the 'FM' prefix). Following withdrawal in the 1960s, it was also purchased and taken to the Stoke Works Junction allotments in Bromsgrove, where on 19 April 1997 it was photographed still in use as an allotment shed.

Southern Railway (SR)

Being the smallest of the four, the SR had far less freight traffic than the others. It was due to this that they did not concentrate on building wagons for carrying containers, but rather decided to build dual-purpose wagons that could also carry cars. These vehicles did not have chains fitted to them, however, so the practice of roping down the containers contained. The number of vehicles hailing from this company to have survived are similar to those found from the GWR and LNER.

Another container that ended up on the Stoke Works Junction allotments was this early 1930s-built SR furniture container, No. K1135S. During 1949, this type of container was re-classified and began to be re-numbered with a BK prefix when they went into works to have maintenance work done on them. Interestingly, the two SR vehicles of this type that I have come across still only bear the K suffix, which means that they were withdrawn before 1952, when the re-numbering process was completed. This one, seen on 19 April 1997, was hidden away in a corner of the allotment, where it was being used as a seed store. Note the bricks it is standing on, which were to keep the rats out.

CHAPTER 18

British Railways Lift On/Off Container Stock

British Railways continued to use the RCH 'standard' designs on their containers (the only difference would be the material used). They also adopted and adapted the GWR 'conflat' idea and these became their standard container-carrying wagons. Bodies of BR-built containers are also found dotted throughout the country but not in as numerous quantities as goods vans.

This plywood container was built at Swindon Works in 1958 and is an insulated container, built especially for the conveyance of frozen foods. Numbered AFB 66414B, it was one of a batch of 100 such containers that operated in a block train between Great Yarmouth and London for the Birdseye Company. It was found at Swithland Sidings on the Great Central Railway on 21 November 2009, where it was partially covered and was awaiting a full restoration.

After the BD general goods containers mentioned in the previous chapter, the second-largest type of containers built were also for general goods and designated as B types; they were identical to the BDs but without the side doors. This example, seen at the Great Central Railway at Loughborough on 21 November 2009, was one of several that were converted and re-designated as BC. The conversion involved the internal fitting of cycle racks and they could carry up to seventy-six bicycles in each one. This example was numbered BC 9900B.

CHAPTER 19

Rescued, Recovered and Restored

Some of the vehicles covered earlier in this book have been recovered and either have been fully restored to their former glory or are awaiting restoration, as have many others not already included. SR, PMV and CCT vehicles tend to make ideal donor underframes and many rescued bodies are now permanently fixed to those vehicles and others which have sometimes been lengthened or shortened accordingly. Some restored bodies have been mounted onto purpose-built, brand-new underframes. The number of recovered bodies has grown substantially in the last few years, with people bequeathing those carriages that have been used as houses, etc. in their wills to preservation societies, heritage railways and museums.

In Chapter One, I included a picture of a London, Chatham & Dover Railway six-wheeled, five-compartment, third-class coach, No. 668, which was in use as a bungalow in Yarcombe, Devon. As I mentioned, that body, and the other LSWR body with it, were moved to the Bluebell Railway following the death of the owner in 2005. Pictured at Sheffield Park shed on the aforementioned preserved railway on 9 October 2016 is the same vehicle, now fully restored and mounted onto an SR covered carriage truck underframe. This vehicle is used on the railway's heritage train service and was used as a carriage again for the first time in June 2016.

Built in 1886 at Highbridge Works on the Somerset & Dorset Joint Railway was this six-wheeled, four-compartment, first-class coach, No. 4. It was withdrawn from service in 1930 and taken to Templecombe, where it was used as a cricket pavilion. It remained there until being purchased by members of the Somerset & Dorset Trust in 1986, and is now based at Washford on the preserved West Somerset Railway. Following its full restoration (which used parts from the S&D body covered in Chapter 1) and fitting the body to a LMSR CCT underframe, it was pictured on 1 August 2015 at Norton Fitzwarren.

Built at Swindon works by the GWR in 1897, for use in the Royal Train during Queen Victoria's Diamond Jubilee, was clerestory-roofed coach No. 233. It was withdrawn in 1930 and its body taken to Aberporth, where it was used as a holiday home until it was rescued in 1982 and fitted to the shortened underframe of a BR carriage. It was on display at Windsor until 2000 when it moved to its current home in the former Swindon Works, where it was pictured on display on 2 June 2012.

In Chapter Seven there is a picture of a GWR TPO vehicle on a remote farm in the Powys countryside. Not long after that picture was taken, the body was taken to the Water Folk Canal Museum at Brecon, where it was used as an office. By March 2006 it was sold to Railholidays UK Ltd at St German's station, in Cornwall, where it was attached to a new purpose-built underframe. It was pictured there on 6 June 2015, in use as holiday accommodation.

No. 23 was built as an open-top, horse-drawn tram by Edinburgh Street Tramways at their works in Shrubhill in 1885. Following its withdrawal from service in 1900, the body was taken to Charlestown, in the Scottish Borders, where it was used as a garden shed. It was to remain there for 106 years, until it was bought in 2006. In 2011 it was taken to the Scottish Vintage Bus Museum at Lathalmond, where it was to undergo a complete restoration. I took this picture on a visit there on 31 March 2013, with it having pride of place on display, complete with photographs showing various stages of its restoration.

If you visit Commercial Street in Dundee, you will come across the Auld Tram Coffee Shop. This rather unique attraction utilises the lower saloon body of an 1882 double-deck Dundee & District Tramway Company steam tram trailer, No.2. In 1899, following its withdrawal, the entire body (both decks) was sold and used as a house until the 1960s, when it was acquired by the Merseyside Tramway Preservation Society. While in storage with them it suffered severe fire damage and the upper deck was totally destroyed; the lower deck fared a little better and was cosmetically restored and put on display at Woodhead Ferry Terminal before being put back into storage, where it remained until space became a premium. In 2007 the body was purchased and converted in Nottingham (at a cost of £45,000) before moving back home to Dundee, where it was placed onto cosmetic looking tram lines and where I photographed it on 28 March 2016.

In Chapter Eleven I featured a Newcastle Corporation Tramways body (No. 117) at Susworth in Lincolnshire. One of the six other bodies that were at that location was the 1901-built Newcastle Corporation Tramways No. 114. Built by Hurst Nelson in Motherwell, its body was taken to Susworth in 1951. In 1987 it was purchased by the Living Open Air Museum of the North at Beamish, where it underwent a complete re-build. It currently sees use on the museum's tramway, as this packed picture from 4 August 2004 clearly shows.